Nick Vandome

Windows 11
Tips, Tricks & Shortcuts

In easy steps is an imprint of In Easy Steps Limited
16 Hamilton Terrace · Holly Walk · Leamington Spa
Warwickshire · United Kingdom · CV32 4LY
www.ineasysteps.com

Notice of Liability
Every effort has been made to ensure that this book contains accurate
and current information. However, In Easy Steps Limited and the
author shall not be liable for any loss or damage suffered by readers
as a result of any information contained herein.

Trademarks
Microsoft® and Windows® are registered trademarks of Microsoft
Corporation. All other trademarks are acknowledged as belonging to
their respective companies.

In Easy Steps Limited supports The Forest Stewardship Council (FSC),
the leading international forest certification organization. All our titles
that are printed on Greenpeace approved FSC certified paper carry the
FSC logo.

MIX
Paper from
responsible sources
FSC® C020837

Printed and bound in the United Kingdom

ISBN 978-1-84078-997-3

Contents

4 Productivity 67

5 Things you can do without 89

6 Customization 97

1 Windows 11 interface

Windows 11 provides a user interface for modern computing needs so that you can get more done, faster. This chapter introduces the Windows 11 operating system, showing how to become familiar with its interface. It also shows how to use some of the less common but still very useful features, the Registry Editor, and the Run commands.

For more information about installing Windows 11, see Chapter 9.

If you do not already have Windows 10 installed on your PC, a clean copy of Windows 11 can still be installed from a DVD. However, this will have to be paid for, rather than a free online upgrade from Windows 10.

Obtaining Windows 11

Windows 11 is an online service, rather than just a stand-alone operating system. This means that by default, Windows 11 is obtained and downloaded online, with subsequent updates and upgrades also provided online on a regular basis.

The main ways of installing Windows 11, for free, are:

- **Using Windows Update** – For upgrading from a previous installed version of Windows 10, retaining the installed applications and settings. This can be done through the **Settings** app (select **Windows Update** and click on the **Check for updates** button).

- **Microsoft website** – Visit the software download page on the Microsoft website (**microsoft.com/en-us/software-download/windows11**) to use the **Windows 11 Installation Assistant** to download Windows 11, as a replacement for an existing version of Windows 10.

- **Preinstalled** – Buy a new PC or laptop with Windows 11 already installed.

Some of the steps that the installation will go through are:

- **Personalize**. These are settings that will be applied to your version of Windows 11. These settings can also be selected within the **Settings** app once Windows 11 has been installed.

- **Settings**. You can choose to have express settings applied, or customize them.

- **Microsoft account**. You can set up a Microsoft account during installation, or once you have started Windows 11.

- **Privacy**. Certain privacy settings can be applied during the setup process for Windows 11.

Signing in

Lock screen

The first thing you'll see when you start up is the Lock screen, which by default shows the time/date, power, and network status. The **Lock screen** is necessary because Windows 11 is a touch-supportive operating system that requires a protective barrier to prevent accidental input. Microsoft has evolved this basic function by enabling users to customize the screen by changing its background and by specifying various notifications, fun facts, tips and tricks to be displayed. This can be done within **Settings** > **Personalization** > **Lock screen**.

For details about accessing the **Settings** app, see page 11.

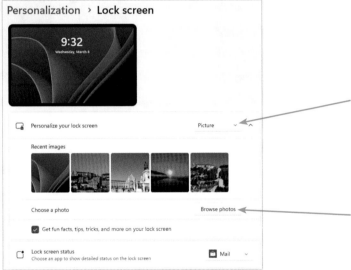

Click in the **Personalize your lock screen** box and select an option from **Picture**, **Slideshow** or **Windows Spotlight**, to use this on the Lock screen. Click the **Browse photos** button to select a photo on your PC to use on the Lock screen.

Sign-in screen

Tap or click anywhere on the Lock screen to reveal the **Sign-in screen**, where you can enter your user password or PIN to sign in.

Sign-in options can be specified in **Settings** > **Accounts** > **Sign-in options**.

Start screen

After signing in to a Windows 11 system you will see the **Start screen** in Desktop mode:

Start screen in Desktop mode

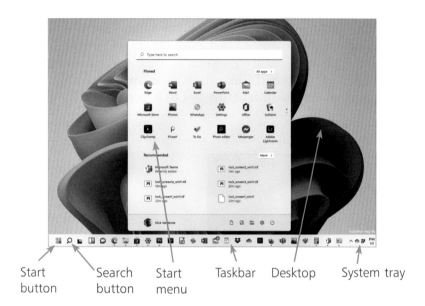

Start button   Search button   Start menu   Taskbar   Desktop   System tray

Click the **Start** button to see the **Start** menu, from where you can access a full list of apps, from the **All apps** button.

The **Start** button is where the **Start** menu can be accessed from. The **Taskbar** remains at the bottom of the screen, regardless of whichever different apps are being used, unless specified otherwise from within the Settings app.

The **system tray** notification area contains icons that give access to:

- **Battery** status and power settings.

- **Network** status and settings.

- **Volume**-level control.

- **Notification Center** for notification messages and system settings.

- **Clock** date and time settings.

- **Show hidden icons**.

Windows 11 can also be used on the Microsoft tablet, known as Microsoft Surface and Surface Pro. These have touchscreen functionality but otherwise their operation is similar to devices using the PC version of Windows 11, which is the one used throughout this book.

Quick tips for getting started

This book is full of tips and tricks for using Windows 11, but here are three that you can use to quickly get up and running:

- Click the **Start** button to access the **Start** menu for accessing all of the apps on your computer and also recently-accessed items.

- Click the **Settings** button on the Taskbar for a huge range of options for customizing the look, feel and functionality of your Windows 11 device.

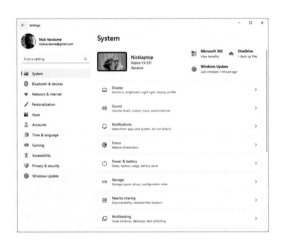

- Click on these three icons in the **system tray** to access the **Quick Settings** panel, which can be used for several tasks, such as connecting to a Wi-Fi network, connecting to Bluetooth, accessing accessibility settings, setting the screen brightness and adjusting the system volume.

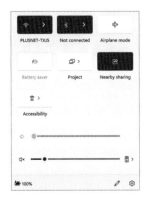

Hot tip

Items in the system tray can be customized in **Settings** > **Personalization** > **Taskbar** > **Other system tray icons**.

Start button

The **Start** button has been a significant part of Windows computing for numerous versions of the operating system. There have been various changes to the **Start** button over the years and it has again been redesigned in Windows 11, with the main difference being it occupies a more central position on the screen, as opposed to being located in the left-hand corner.

Using the Start button

The **Start** button provides access to the apps on your Windows 11 computer and also to the enhanced Start menu.

1   Click on the **Start** button at the bottom left-hand side of the Taskbar

2   The **Start** menu is displayed

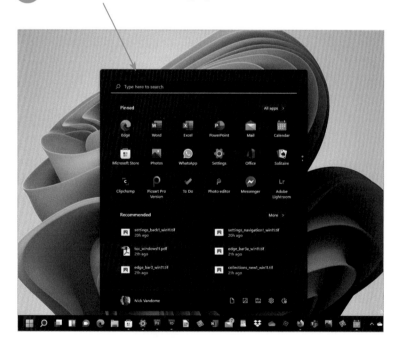

3   The Start menu contains access to all of the apps on your computer, and also recommended items

4   Other items can also be accessed from the **Start** button by right-clicking on it; see page 18

Hot tip

Items on the Start menu can be customized from the **Personalization > Start** section of the Settings app. The Start menu and the Taskbar can be viewed in either **Dark** or **Light** mode, which can be selected in **Personalization > Colors > Choose your mode.**

Hot tip

Click on the **Power** button on the Start menu to access options for **Sleep**, **Shut down** or **Restart**.

12

Repositioning the Start button

Although the **Start** button has moved into a more central position, along with the Taskbar, it is still possible to restore it to the left-hand corner, if desired. This is done by moving the whole of the Taskbar to the left. To do this:

1 Click on the **Settings** app on the Taskbar or the Start menu

2 Click on the **Personalization** tab

3 Click on the **Taskbar** option

4 Click on the **Taskbar behaviors** option

Taskbar behaviors
Taskbar alignment, badging, automatically hide, and multiple displays

13

5 Click here in the **Taskbar alignment** panel to select options for how the Taskbar is aligned

6 Click on the **Left** option to align the Taskbar to the left-hand side, situating the **Start** button in the left-hand corner

Left

Center

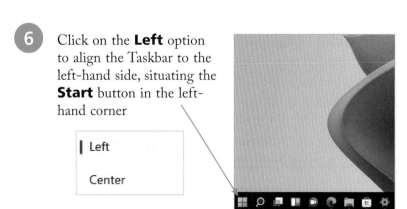

In Step 6, all of the icons on the Taskbar are aligned to the left, in addition to the **Start** button.

Start menu

The **Start** menu has been a permanent fixture in Windows, but its appearance and functionality have changed significantly over the years. This evolution continues with Windows 11, with a newly-designed Start menu. This is where you can access areas within your computer, perform certain functions, and also access apps from a variety of locations. To use the Start menu:

 Click on the **Start** button to access the **Start** menu. **Pinned** apps are shown at the top of the Start menu, with **Recommended** items below. Click on an item to open it

Some of the default items on the bottom toolbar of the Start menu can be customized to a certain extent (see page 17).

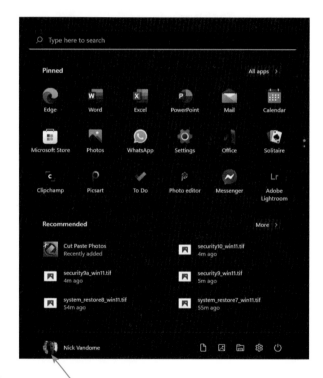

The options in Step 3 can also be accessed by right-clicking on the **Start** button and clicking on the **Shut down or sign out** button.

Click here to access your own account settings or sign out from your account

Click on the **Power** button for options to **Sleep** your computer, **Shut down** or **Restart**

14

4 Click on the **All apps** button at the top of the **Pinned** section, to view all of the apps on your computer

5 Scroll up and down the **All apps** section to view the available apps. Click on one to open it

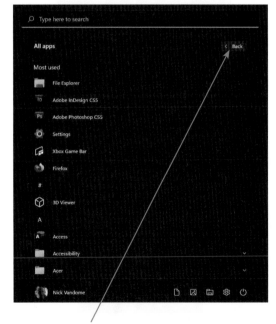

6 Click on the **Back** button in the top right-hand corner of the **All apps** panel, to go back to the main Start menu

...cont'd

7 On the **All apps** screen, click on one of the alphabetic headings; e.g. B

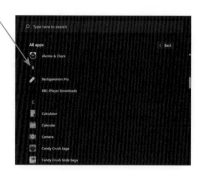

16

8 An alphabetic grid is displayed

9 Click on a character on the alphabetic grid to go to the relevant section

Customizing the Start menu

Windows 11 is very adaptable and can be customized in several ways so that it works best for you. This includes the Start menu, which can be set to behave in certain ways and have specific items added to it. To do this:

1 Click on the **Settings** app on the Taskbar

2 Click on the **Personalization** tab

3 Click on the **Start** option

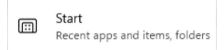

4 Under **Start**, select whether to show recently-added apps, show most-used apps, or show recently-opened items, on the Start menu

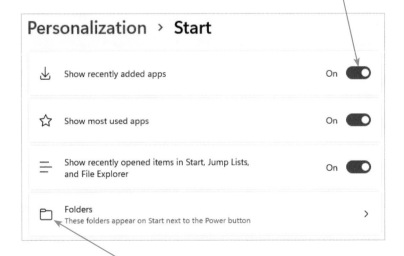

5 Click on the **Folders** option to select items that appear on the Start menu

Recently-added and most-used apps appear at the top of the **All apps** section of the Start menu, if these options are turned **On**.

17

More menus

Power User menu

Right-click on the **Start** button to open the Power User menu – a menu of options likely to be of interest to advanced users:

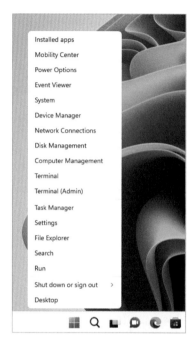

Installed apps
Mobility Center
Power Options
Event Viewer
System
Device Manager
Network Connections
Disk Management
Computer Management
Terminal
Terminal (Admin)
Task Manager
Settings
File Explorer
Search
Run
Shut down or sign out   >
Desktop

You can also open the Power User menu by pressing **WinKey** + **X**.

Task View

Click the **Task View** button to reveal a thumbnail of each open app on the Start screen:

You can also open **Task View** by pressing **WinKey** + **Tab**.

Windows' **Task List** can also be used to show open apps by holding down the **Alt** key then pressing the **Tab** key.

Tap or click to select the app you want to work with, or press **WinKey** + **Tab** again to close Task View.

Navigation

In its drive for Windows 11 to be all-encompassing, Microsoft has made it possible to navigate the interface in three different ways: by touchpad (touch), the mouse, and the keyboard.

Touch

Touch gestures, for devices that support this functionality, include swiping, sliding, tapping, and pinching. The best way to get to grips with these is to experiment. The following, however, will get you off to a good start:

Tap – Opens, selects or activates whatever you tap (similar to clicking with a mouse).

Tap and hold – Shows further information about an item or opens a context menu (similar to right-clicking with a mouse).

Pinch or stretch – Visually zooms in or out, like on a website, map or picture.

Rotate – Some items can be rotated by placing your fingers on them and turning your hand.

Slide to scroll – Dragging your finger across the screen scrolls through items (similar to scrolling a mouse wheel).

Slide to arrange – Drag an item around the screen with your finger to position it (similar to dragging with a mouse).

Swipe to select – A short, quick movement will select an item and often bring up app commands.

Swipe or slide from right edge – Opens the Notification Center.

Swipe or slide from left edge – Opens the Task View feature.

Swipe or slide from top edge – Enables you to view the title bar in full-screen apps.

Swipe or slide from bottom edge – Enables you to view the Taskbar in full-screen apps.

In many cases, the touch commands available are dependent on the application in use. For example, various rotational commands can be used to manipulate objects in drawing and layout applications such as Microsoft PowerPoint.

Beware

Touch gestures do not work with all touchpads, and they generally work best with precision touchpads. To check this, look in **Settings > Bluetooth & devices > Touchpad**.

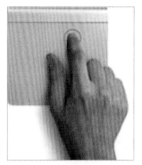

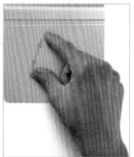

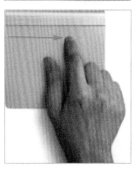

Hot tip

Spinning the mouse wheel while on the **Lock screen** will open the **Sign-in screen**.

...cont'd

Mouse

Using the mouse to get around in Windows 11 is no different from any other operating system. The trick is knowing where to position the mouse to reveal the menus and features provided by the interface.

Keyboard

Those of you who use the Start screen without the benefit of a touchscreen are well advised to get acquainted with the various keyboard commands relevant to it. In many cases, just as with keyboard commands and shortcuts in general, they are often quicker than using the mouse.

There are actually a whole bunch of these commands – a full list is shown on pages 148-150. The following are some of the more useful ones:

An important key is the Windows key, also called **WinKey**. Pressing this key instantly opens the Start screen menu regardless of where the user is. It can also be used in conjunction with other keys to perform other actions. For example, **WinKey** + **X** opens the **Power User** menu, as shown on page 18.

The **Home** and **End** keys jump to the beginning or the end of a line of text. The **Enter** key activates a highlighted action; e.g. if a button is highlighted in a dialog window.

WinKey + **Tab** opens a **Task View** list that allows the user to switch to a different app – by scrolling through thumbnails using the arrow keys, then pressing the **Enter** key to select an open app.

Holding down the **Alt** key then pressing **Tab** opens a horizontal **Task List**. You can move between thumbnails by pressing **Tab** then release **Alt** to open the selected app. Note you must have at least two apps running for **WinKey** + **Tab** and **Alt** + **Tab** to work.

A rarely-used key known as the **Context Menu** key (usually located close to the space bar) brings up a menu of related options when pressed in an open app. The context menu typically appears at the top of the app window.

Run commands

Run commands won't concern the majority of Windows users, but if you are looking to get more out of your computing experience and delve slightly deeper into Windows 11, it is an excellent option for accessing a range of functions that you might not otherwise come across. Run commands are used at appropriate points in the book and they can be accessed as follows:

1 Right-click the **Start** button and click the **Run** button on the Power User menu

The **Run** dialog window can also be accessed by pressing **WinKey** + **R** on the keyboard.

2 A **Run** dialog window appears

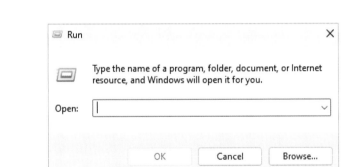

3 Enter the required command into the **Open** text box and click the **OK** button

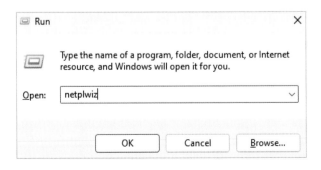

The Control Panel

The **Control Panel** has been part of numerous versions of Windows, providing access to a range of useful functions that can be applied to the operation of a Windows PC. However, as Windows has evolved, many of the functions of the Control Panel have been moved to the Settings app, particularly with Windows 10 and then Windows 11. Despite this, the Control Panel remains a valuable resource for a number of options, particularly if you want to go a little bit deeper into the inner workings of Windows.

The Control Panel is referenced to in various places throughout the book, and it is important to be aware of it and how to get the most out of it. To do this:

The **Windows Tools** option is another important one for anyone looking to develop their skills with Windows 11.

1   Click the **Start** button, click the **All apps** button and click the **Windows Tools** button on the **Start** menu

Windows Tools

2   Double-click the **Control Panel** button in the **Windows Tools** window

Control Panel

To make the Control Panel readily available, it can be pinned to the Taskbar so that it is always a click away. To do this, right-click on the **Control Panel** icon in Step 2 and click the **Pin to taskbar** option.

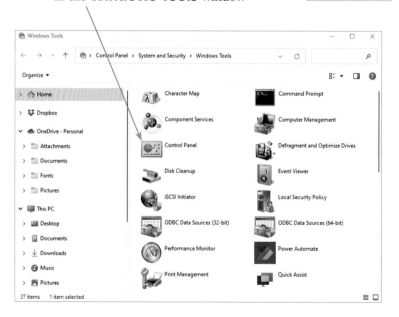

3 The main Control Panel categories are displayed, with some of the sub-categories listed below the main headings

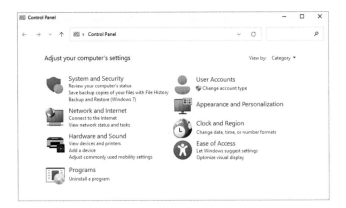

As you move through the categories and sub-categories of the Control Panel, the location is shown in the address bar at the top of the window.

4 Click one of the main categories to view the items within it, and access their functionality by clicking on them

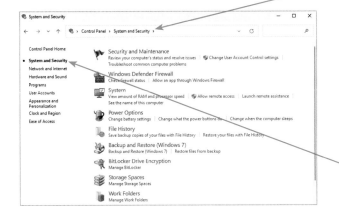

Use the left-hand sidebar to move to the other main categories within the Control Panel, or back to the homepage.

5 Click in the **View by** box in Step 3 to access options for how the Control Panel is displayed

6 Select an option for displaying items within the Control Panel

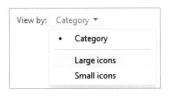

The **View by: Large icons/Small icons** option displays all items within the Control Panel, rather than just the main categories.

Registry Editor

Another important function that appears throughout the book is the **Registry Editor**. This is an option within Windows where more advanced users can make changes to some of the inner workings of Windows that are not immediately obvious to most general users. It can be used to make administration-level changes, such as changing permissions for users and changing various hardware and software configurations. Some of these options are listed in the book, with instructions of how to use and navigate the Registry Editor. However, it is useful to be aware of its locations and how it operates. To do this:

Hot tip

As with the Control Panel, it is a good idea to pin the Registry Editor to the Taskbar so that it is readily available. To do this, access the **Registry Editor** icon in Step 1 and click the **Pin to taskbar** option.

1 Access Windows Tools, as shown on page 22, and double-click the **Registry Editor** option, or right-click the **Start** button and click the **Run** option. In the **Run** dialog box, enter **regedit** and click the **OK** button

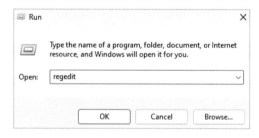

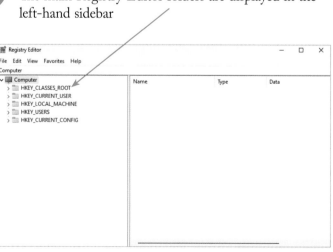

2 The main Registry Editor folders are displayed in the left-hand sidebar

3 Click the main folders in the left-hand sidebar to expand them. Keep doing this with sub-folders, as required, until you can locate the folder that you need

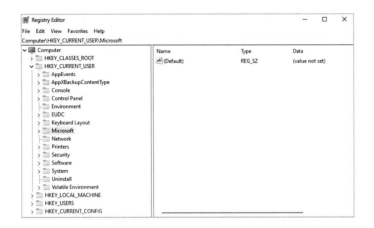

4 To use the functionality of the Registry Editor, different strings and values usually have to be accessed or set. To do this, right-click on an item in the right-hand window and select **New** > **Key**

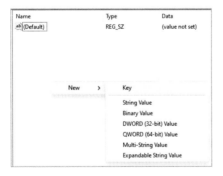

5 Enter a value, as required, and click the **OK** button (relevant values for the Registry Editor will be noted throughout the book, where they are required)

Apps

Windows 11 comes with a number of useful apps for productivity and entertainment. In addition, there are thousands more available from the Microsoft Store.

Many of these apps display content in real time. For example, there is a **Weather** app that shows a constantly-updated 10-day forecast and a **News** app that displays current stories and images.

These apps are user-friendly and simple. As with the Windows 11 interface itself, Microsoft has designed the apps to be clean and straightforward with the minimum of extraneous clutter – the app's content is intended to dominate. A consequence of this is that traditional navigational aids such as toolbars, menus, and preview panes are in evidence to a much lesser degree.

To use Microsoft terminology, the Universal Windows apps are "immersive applications" – which basically means they run best in full-screen mode. For users with a large, wide-screen monitor, this is definitely a restriction. However, this is mitigated to a certain extent by a feature called **Snap**. This makes it possible to have up to four apps running side by side – see pages 84-85 for details.

Traditional Windows apps, such as **Notepad**, will still work in Windows 11. It's important to be aware that Universal Windows apps are different from their traditional Windows equivalents.

Sourcing and installing apps

In order to provide as secure a computing environment as possible, official Windows 11 apps are only available from the Microsoft Store. This effectively "sandboxes" them and, as a result, users are much less likely to introduce viruses and malware to their computers via downloaded software.

To access the Microsoft Store, click the **Microsoft Store** icon on the Taskbar or on the Start menu. You will then be asked to sign in with your Microsoft account.

Hot tip

It is possible to install third-party apps on Windows 11 – see page 47.

Microsoft Store

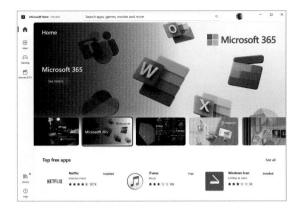

The first things you see on the **Home** screen are promoted apps and four category buttons in the left-hand sidebar for **Home**, **Apps**, **Gaming**, and **Movies & TV**.

At the top of the window is a Search box that can locate an app by keyword. Using the sections, screens or search takes you to the app's

page where there are typically **Screenshots**, a **Description**, and **Ratings and reviews**. Below the app's title is an install button labeled **Free** or with the purchase price. Once you've chosen an app, and paid if required, click the install button to download the app and see it appear on the Start menu's A-Z list.

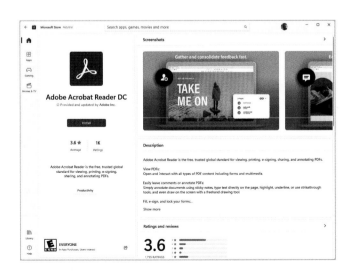

Selecting any "Top..." category in the Store provides a filter to refine your search.

Check out its **Ratings and reviews** before choosing an app.

By using the same Microsoft account, all official apps installed on your PC will also be available on any other Windows 11 devices you may have.

27

...cont'd

Closing apps

Closing an app is very simple to do, but it must be pointed out that usually it is not actually necessary to close apps. This is because when a new app is opened, other running apps are switched to a state of suspension in which they use very little in the way of system resources.

However, there may be situations in which it is desirable or even necessary to close down an app. Here are five ways to do this:

- Simply press **Alt + F4** – this kills the app instantly.

- Click or tap the **X** (**Close**) button on the app window's title bar.

- Right-click the app in **Task View** and select **Close**.

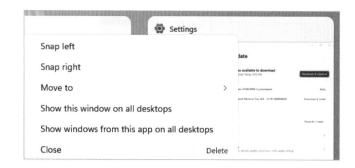

- Right-click the app icon on the Taskbar and select **Close all windows** in the pop-up context menu that appears.

- Press **Ctrl + Shift + Esc** to open **Task Manager**, then right-click to select the app and click the **End task** option.

2 Performance

Windows operating systems require a powerful computer in order to function at their best. Those of you whose systems are struggling to run Windows 11 will be able to achieve a higher level of performance by implementing the measures described in this chapter. The chapter also explains some more general performance-boosting steps that apply to Windows so that you can get it running to the very best of its capabilities and at maximum efficiency.

Overview

Operating systems, no matter how good they may be, are completely reliant on the hardware used to run them. If the hardware is not up to the job, while the operating system may function, it will not do so at its best.

Even where the hardware is good enough, if it is configured or installed incorrectly, the operating system will be adversely affected. On a slightly different tack, it is often possible to squeeze a bit more performance from a hardware device by tweaking its settings.

In this chapter, we look at these issues and show how to get both your computer and operating system running at their maximum performance level.

Your hardware is the place to start.

However, if you do experience any problems, or would simply like to get your computer running as well as possible, there are quite a few adjustments that can be made to the default settings, which will make it run considerably faster. For users whose hardware provides a performance level that is on the borderline between poor and acceptable, these can negate the need for a hardware upgrade.

There are also some more general steps that users can take in order to keep their system running, not just at peak performance but also reliably. These are not specific to Windows 11 – they apply to any operating system.

This chapter shows the tweaks that can be made to Windows 11's default settings to improve its performance, and also shows, generally, how to keep your PC running smoothly and reliably.

Please note that in this book, unless otherwise mentioned, we are concentrating on the Windows Desktop mode interface, as is used on traditional mouse-controlled desktop PCs, rather than the Windows 11 Tablet mode interface, which is really only suitable for handheld devices and touchscreen monitors.

If your system struggles with Windows 11, there are steps you can take to reduce the demands made by it.

Adding more memory

Without doubt, the quickest and most effective method of improving the overall performance of any computer is to simply increase the amount of its Random Access Memory (RAM). Windows 11 will not function well with any less than 1GB of memory. Optimum performance will require 2GB.

Adding memory is a simple procedure that takes no more than a few minutes, but does require the system case to be opened. On a PC this reveals the motherboard containing the memory modules:

Open the retaining clips at the ends of an empty memory socket, then insert a new memory module by gently pressing down on the top edge until the clips close automatically.

On a laptop computer you can find an access panel on the underside of the case that reveals the memory modules. Push apart the retaining clips until the socket pops up.

If one or more of the sockets are empty, all you have to do is fit extra modules to complement the existing ones. If the sockets are all in use, you will have to remove some, or all, of the modules and replace them with modules of a larger capacity.

However, if the prospect of meddling inside the case doesn't appeal to you there is an easier, although less effective, option available called **ReadyBoost**, which is explained on page 32.

Hot tip

To discover how much memory your PC has, press **WinKey** + **R** then type **msinfo32** into the **Run** box to open the **System Information Summary**, and then scroll down to the **Total Physical Memory** item.

Don't forget

You cannot install just any memory – it has to be compatible. Check online to see which type you need.

Beware

Memory modules must be handled very carefully. Before touching one, ground yourself by touching the metal case chassis. If you don't, the electrostatic charge in your body could well damage the module.

Quick speed boost

If Windows were to run out of memory, the system would grind to a halt. To prevent this, it uses a "paging file" on the hard drive as a memory substitute. The problem with this is that hard drives are much slower than memory, so performance is reduced when the paging file is being used.

The solution is to prevent Windows from having to use the paging file, and the way to do this is to install more memory. However, many users don't know how to install memory – plus, it is expensive.

ReadyBoost provides an easier and cheaper alternative – you just need a USB flash drive with a capacity between 256MB and 4GB.

Hot tip

The minimum amount of flash memory you can use for **ReadyBoost** is 256MB. The maximum amount is 4GB.

1 Connect the USB drive then right-click its icon in **File Explorer** and select **Properties** from the context menu

2 In the **Properties** dialog, choose the **ReadyBoost** tab

3 Now, select **Dedicate this device to ReadyBoost**

4 Click **OK** to create a ReadyBoost cache file in the USB drive

Don't forget

ReadyBoost enables you to increase your system's performance without having to buy and install more memory. It is also a much cheaper option, as flash drives are half the price of memory of equivalent capacity.

Windows will now use the USB drive as a cache for the most commonly-paged data. The paging file will still be on the hard drive but will be used much less.

Reducing visual effects

Windows comes with a number of visual effects such as fading or sliding menus, drop shadows, and pointer shadows. These are all designed to improve the look and feel of the Windows interface.

They do, however, add nothing to its functionality. In fact, they can – and do – have a negative impact on the system. Remember that each of these effects consumes system resources.

Users interested in performance rather than appearance will benefit from disabling some, or even all of these essentially unnecessary graphic enhancements.

1 Right-click on the **Start** button, to open the **Power User** menu. Click on the **System** option to open this in the **Settings** app. Click on the **Advanced system settings** option, in the **Related links** section

Related links   Domain or workgroup   System protection   Advanced system settings

2 Click on the **Advanced** tab and click on the **Settings...** button in the **Performance** section

3 Now, check **On** the **Adjust for best performance** option

4 By default, Windows chooses the first option, **Let Windows choose what's best for my computer**, which enables the majority of the effects. You can disable them all, as shown in Step 3 above. Alternatively, you can disable them individually

Icon thumbnails

By default, Windows displays all file icons as thumbnails (mini graphical representations). This is particularly useful when viewing image files, as it enables you to see the image without having to first open it in an imaging app, as shown below:

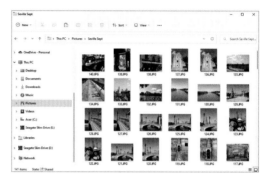

Graphic files are the slowest file type to load – thumbnails are small, but their negative effect on system performance is cumulative.

However, there is a downside. Because graphic files take longer to open than any other type of file, having this feature enabled does adversely affect system performance. Users who want their system to run as fast as possible, and those who simply need a performance boost, will benefit by disabling this feature. Do it as described below:

1 Open the **Settings** app and enter **file explorer options** into the **Search** box and click on the result

Check **On** the **Show hidden files, folders, and drives** option shown here to ensure **File Explorer** provides a comprehensive view of your system contents.

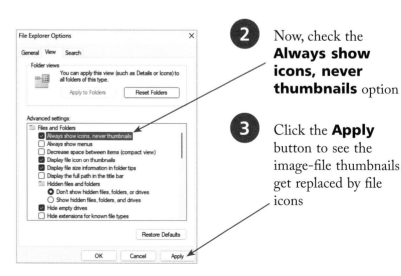

2 Now, check the **Always show icons, never thumbnails** option

3 Click the **Apply** button to see the image-file thumbnails get replaced by file icons

Faster paging

When Windows runs out of physical memory it uses a special file on the hard drive as a substitute, known as the paging file. Moving it to a different drive speeds up the paging operation, and thus system performance (see the first Hot tip). To carry out this procedure you will, of course, need two hard drives.

1 Access System Properties and click on **Advanced** > **Performance** > **Settings...**, as shown on page 33

2 Click on the **Advanced** tab and click on the **Change...** button in the **Virtual memory** section

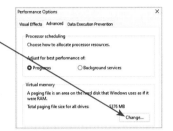

3 Uncheck the **Automatically manage paging file size for all drives** option

4 Next, select the **No paging file** option

5 Now, click the **Set** button. Ignore the warning message and click **Yes** to continue

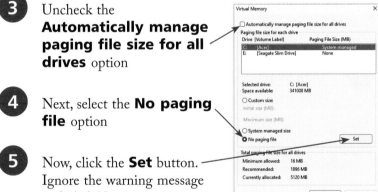

6 Select a different drive

7 Select **System managed size**

8 Click **Set** and then click **OK**. Reboot your computer to apply the change

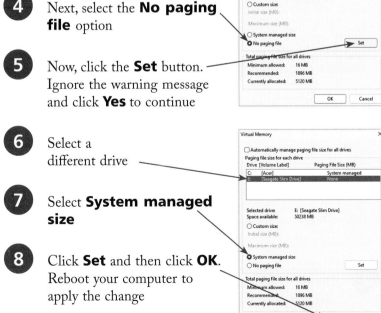

A separate drive that doesn't have Windows and other applications installed on it will be more responsive as it has used much less space than the main drive. So, placing the paging file on it will improve the speed of the paging operation.

The **Custom size** option lets you choose an initial size and a maximum size for the paging file.

There is no benefit to be gained by moving the paging file to a different partition on the same drive. It must be moved to a separate drive.

Disk thrashing occurs on PCs that are low on memory, which causes the operating system to frequently utilize the hard drive as a memory substitute. This leads to data being constantly transferred between the hard drive and the memory.

Beware

Disk thrashing can damage or cause premature failure of the hard drive due to excessive wear and tear on the read/write heads.

Hot tip

Systems with solid state drives (SSD) may see little, if any, advantage with Superfetch – due to their performance advantage over regular hard disk drives (HDD).

Disabling Superfetch

The **Superfetch** feature in Windows helps to keep the computer consistently responsive to your apps, by making better use of the computer's memory.

Superfetch prioritizes the apps you're currently using over background tasks, and also adapts to the way you work by tracking the apps you use most often and preloading these into memory. As a result, they open much more quickly when accessed.

On PCs that have 2GB or more of memory, **Superfetch** works very well. However, if your PC has less than 2GB it can lead to excessive disk thrashing (see the first Hot tip) and sluggish system performance. The less memory you have, the worse the effect.

If you find yourself in this position, you have three options:

- Upgrade your memory so that you have at least 2GB.

- Enable **ReadyBoost** – see page 32.

- Disable the **Superfetch** feature (via the **SysMain** section).

The latter is done as follows:

1 Go to **Start** > **All apps** > **Windows Tools**. Double-click **Services** and scroll down to **SysMain**

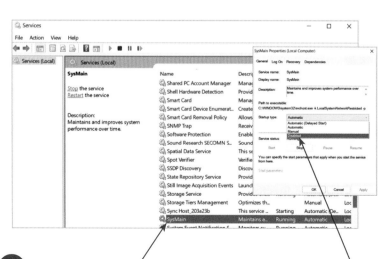

2 Double-click **SysMain**, to open its **Properties** dialog, and in the **Startup type** drop-down box select **Disabled**

Canceling unneeded services

When a Windows PC is being used, in the background and unseen by the user, a number of applications known as "services" will be running. While many of them are essential for certain functions of the operating system, there are some that are not.

As every running application makes a hit on system performance, this is something you will want to prevent. Fortunately, you can override Windows and make a decision yourself as to which services should be running. As a guide, those services specified in the list on the right can be disabled safely. The procedure for doing so is exactly the same as described on the previous page (**Disabling Superfetch**).

However, should you consider disabling any services that are not listed on the right, we suggest that you first take a look at what the service does and also which other applications may be depending on it. Do this as follows:

1 Access **Windows Tools** > **Services** and right-click on a service to open the its **Properties** dialog box, where you will see a description of the service's function

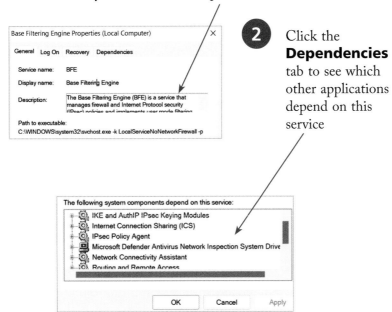

2 Click the **Dependencies** tab to see which other applications depend on this service

By checking this out, you will not inadvertently disable a service that is essential to the running of your PC.

Hot tip

Services that can be safely disabled are:

- **IKE and AuthIP IPsec Keying Modules**
- **Remote Registry**
- **UPnP Device Host**
- **WebClient**
- **Windows Error Reporting Service**
- **Windows Image Acquisition (WIA)**

If you don't use your PC for networking, the following services can also be disabled:

- **Computer Browser**
- **Distributed Link Tracking Client**
- **Netlogon**
- **Peer Name Resolution Protocol**
- **Peer Networking Identity Manager**
- **SSDP Discovery**
- **Server**
- **TCP/IP NetBIOS Helper**
- **Workstation**

More shutdown options

There are several ways to access the Windows 11 power-off options: by clicking the **Start** button then **Power**; by right-clicking the **Start** button, then **Shut down or sign out**; or by clicking the **Power** button on the **Lock** screen.

Here is another way that provides **Shut down**, **Switch user**, **Sign out**, **Sleep**, and **Restart** options:

1. Type **notepad** into the Taskbar **Search** box then hit **Enter** – to open the **Windows Notepad** application

2. In **Notepad**, precisely type the following:
```
dim objShell
set objShell = CreateObject("shell.application")
objShell.ShutdownWindows
set objShell = nothing
```

3. From the file menu, click **Save As**, and in the box enter a suitable name; e.g. **Shutdown**. Give it the **.vbs** file extension as shown below and save it to the desktop

4. Double-click the **Shutdown** icon that now appears on the desktop, to see a **Shut Down Windows** dialog box offering Windows 11 power-off options:

This example creates a handy shutdown script using the **Visual Basic** scripting language called **VBScript**.

The quotation marks in the script in Step 2 need to be straight ones, not curly ones, in order for the script to work.

You can drag your new **Shutdown** icon to the Taskbar where it can be quickly accessed.

Streamlining the Registry

The Registry is a central hierarchical database that holds all of the important Windows settings regarding software, hardware and system configuration. It also provides a common location for all applications to save their launching parameters and data.

Over time, as the user installs and deletes apps, creates shortcuts and changes system settings etc., obsolete and invalid key information builds up in the Registry. While this does not have a major impact on a PC's performance, it can be the cause of system and app errors that can lead to instability issues.

The solution is to scan the Registry periodically with a suitable application that will locate all invalid entries and delete them.

While Windows Registry Editor is adequate for editing purposes, it does not provide a cleaning option. However, there are many such utilities available for download from the internet. A typical example is **CCleaner** (shown below). These apps provide various options, such as full or selective scans, backups, and the creation of **System Restore Points**.

A free version of the **CCleaner** utility can be downloaded from ccleaner.com/

The **CCleaner** utility can also be used to clean out accumulated junk, such as temporary files, to keep your system running well.

Occasional use of a Registry cleaner helps keep your system stable and reliable. CCleaner also provides active monitoring to notify you when your system would benefit from a clean.

Optimizing the hard drive

Assuming you're not already using one, a very good way of improving not only drive performance but also that of the whole PC is to replace the boot hard drive (the one Windows is installed on) with a solid state drive (SSD).

Hot tip

The ideal way to use an SSD is to set it up as the boot drive and use a cheaper mechanical hard drive for data storage.

Replacing the boot hard drive will mean opening up the system case, which is something many users will not be comfortable with. However, if you are prepared to do it, or know someone who can do it for you, the benefits are considerable. The main one is speed – the "seek" time of an SSD (the time it takes to locate a file) is in the order of .01 ms compared to around 7 ms for a traditional mechanical hard drive. The result is a computer in which boot times are typically halved and apps open instantaneously.

Don't forget

Windows 11 provides **TRIM** support that automatically cleans your SSD – to ensure its performance does not degrade with use.

SSDs are also far more reliable than mechanical drives as they contain no moving parts. This means it is much safer to store data on an SSD. Other advantages include their small dimensions, low power requirements, and no need for maintenance (defragmentation).

The only real drawbacks of these devices is the cost – two to three times as much as a mechanical drive, and relatively low storage capacity. For these reasons, the use of SSDs is usually restricted to the boot drive, with a mechanical drive providing much larger and cheaper data storage capacity.

Hot tip

Most SSD manufacturers offer free tools to manage and optimize their SSDs, such as the **Intel SSD Toolbox**. Check out the manufacturer's website of your own SSD.

Installing an SSD is actually a very simple operation. All that is required is to secure the device in place, then connect the data and power cables to the drive. You'll also need to install a clean copy of the operating system on the drive, or copy it from the existing drive. Full installation and setup instructions are usually supplied with the devices.

Keeping it lean and mean

When approximately 70% of a hard drive's storage capacity has been used, its performance level will start to decrease. It will also be more likely to be affected by the issue of fragmentation.

So, when it begins to approach this mark, you should start thinking about freeing up some space. As it's a sure fact that many of the files on your drive will be redundant, you can usually do this without losing anything important.

The more data you have on your drive, the worse the effects of fragmentation.

1 Access the **Windows Tools** app on the **All apps** list from the **Start** menu and double-click on the **Disk Cleanup** option to scan the file system

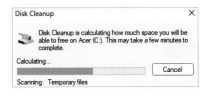

2 Under **Files to delete** you will see a list of all files that can be safely deleted. Check the required boxes and then click **OK** to delete them

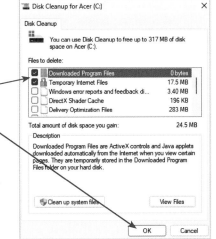

3 Click **Clean up system files**. You'll see a list of system files that can be deleted. Delete these as described above

System Restore Points are created whenever major changes are made to the system. These points can occupy a tremendous amount of disk space, so deleting them is worth doing. The actions on the left delete all but the most recent **Restore Point**.

The next thing to delete is **System Restore Points**. As these are actually system backups, they are very large files, often several GB in size, and there may be several of them. Click **Clean up system files**, then select the **More Options** tab and click **Clean up** under **System Restore and Shadow Copies**.

Finally, click **Clean up** under **Apps and Features**. You'll see a list of all apps installed on the PC. Go through the list and uninstall any that you don't use. You'll now have even more free disk space.

...cont'd

Keeping the file system healthy

Over time, especially if the PC is well used, file system and data faults can build up on the hard drive. Not only can these have an adverse effect on the PC's performance, but they can also be the cause of general system instability, and thus potential loss of data.

To correct these types of faults, Windows provides a disk maintenance utility called **chkdsk** (check disk). Access it as follows:

1 Press **WinKey + X** to open the Power User menu. Select **File Explorer**, then choose **This PC**

2 Right-click the drive you want to check, and select **Properties**. In the dialog box, click the **Tools** tab

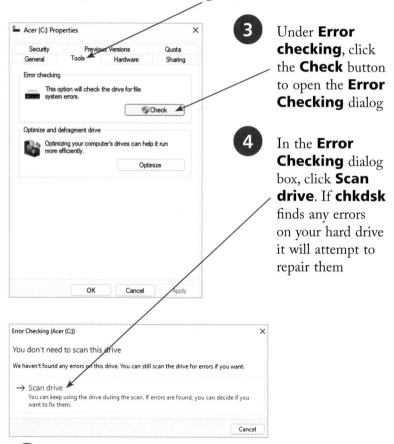

3 Under **Error checking**, click the **Check** button to open the **Error Checking** dialog

4 In the **Error Checking** dialog box, click **Scan drive**. If **chkdsk** finds any errors on your hard drive it will attempt to repair them

5 Upon completion, **chkdsk** reports **Your drive was successfully scanned**

Defragmenting

Another important piece of housekeeping for your computer's hard drive is to defragment (defrag) it on a regular basis.

1 Access the **This PC** > **Properties** > **Tools** window, as shown on the previous page

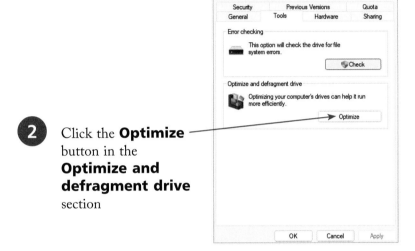

2 Click the **Optimize** button in the **Optimize and defragment drive** section

Defragmenting is required because, over time, data in files becomes broken up (fragmented) and stored in different locations on your computer from where it was originally stored. This means that is takes the computer longer to retrieve the data when it is required. After defragmenting, the data should be returned to its original location.

3 Select a drive on your computer and click the **Analyze** button to check whether it needs to be optimized. Click the **Optimize** button to begin the optimization process, which will defragment the selected drive, ensuring that it works more efficiently

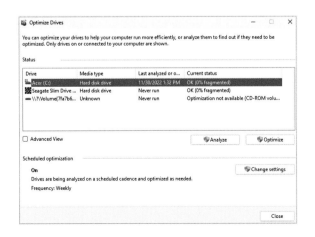

Upgrading your device drivers is not just important for the operating system – in many cases, the devices will then perform better too.

Hot tip

If Windows freezes, or is producing frequent Stop errors, check if the problem is being caused by a faulty driver.

Hot tip

Drivers that are certified for use with Windows have been tested by Windows Hardware Quality Labs (WHQL). They are commonly referred to as "signed drivers" as they have been digitally tagged as such.

Updating device drivers

What exactly is a driver? Well, let's assume that you are about to print a document and have opened your printer software to change a few settings. What you are looking at is actually a driver – in this case, your printer's driver. A driver has three purposes:

- First, some drivers, like the printer driver mentioned above, act as an interface between the device and the user – allowing changes to be made to the way the device operates.

- Second, all drivers act as an interface between their device and the operating system. They tell the operating system which system resources the device needs for correct operation.

- Third, drivers provide a way for hardware manufacturers to update their devices to take account of advances in technology, both hardware and software.

Unfortunately, drivers can cause problems, particularly when they are used with a new operating system (this invariably introduces technologies that the driver's devices were not designed for). In most cases they will install without problems and the devices will appear to be functioning. However, behind the scenes the drivers may well be the cause of incompatibility issues that can lead to both instability and loss of system performance.

In an effort to prevent this, Windows displays a warning message when it detects that a potentially problematic driver is being installed. However, it is a fact that most users ignore these messages and install the driver regardless. If you've done this yourself, you should be aware that you may well have compromised your system.

So, to be quite sure that the PC is running at its best, you must uninstall all non-certified Windows drivers and replace them with ones that are certified. To do this:

1 Go to the **Search** box on the Taskbar and type **verifier**

2 Click the **Verifier** search result, then click **Yes**

...cont'd

3 Select **Create standard settings** and click **Next**

4 In the next dialog box, select **Automatically select unsigned drivers** and click **Next**

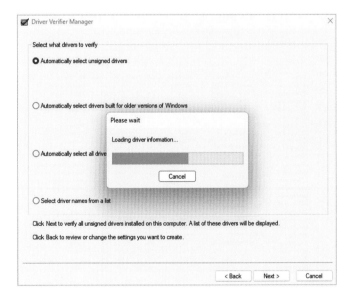

If the search discovers any unsigned drivers, they will be listed for you to verify. While they may be fine, these drivers are all potential causes of system problems. Therefore, if you want to be absolutely certain that your computer is stable and performing as well as possible, you will have to either replace them all with Windows-certified versions or uninstall them.

To this end, visit the websites of the devices' manufacturers and look for updated drivers certified for use with Windows 11. Download and install them. If a manufacturer doesn't provide a Windows 11 driver, ideally you should replace the device with one from a manufacturer that does.

Many users assume that system crashes and lockups are due to faults in the operating system. The reality is that the majority of them are caused by uncertified hardware drivers or low-quality memory.

45

Corrupt signed drivers may also cause problems. Choose the **Select driver names from a list** option to verify individual drivers.

Prioritizing CPU resources

"Priority" is the measure that Windows uses to determine the amount of Central Processing Unit (CPU) time that each application receives. By default, most apps are set to the **Normal** priority level, so by changing a specific app to a higher level you can effectively boost its performance. This is useful when you are using several applications simultaneously (multitasking).

1 Run the app to be prioritized then open **Task Manager** (**Ctrl** + **Shift** + **Esc**)

2 Click the menu icon in the top left-hand corner and click the **Details** option

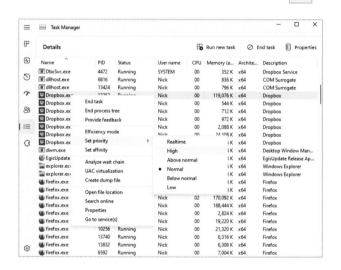

3 Right-click on the app you want to prioritize and select **Set priority** to see options ranging from **Low** to **Realtime** priority level

4 Select the priority level you want for that application, then click **Change priority** and close **Task Manager**

Note that changes to priority levels are not permanent; they are effective only while the app is running. If you close the app and then open it again, it will have reverted to the default setting.

Beware

The highest-priority setting is **Realtime**. This will give an application the same priority as critical system services. We recommend that you do NOT use this, as doing so can render your system unstable.

Don't forget

You can also set lower-priority levels for your applications.

Hot tip

If you have an open app that is accessed infrequently, giving it a lower priority will increase the CPU resources available for more frequently-used applications.

Third-party software

Having tweaked Windows to give improved performance, you should now look at your PC's applications. These can also be the cause of performance issues.

App overload
The first thing to examine is the number of apps you have installed. The more there are, the slower your PC is going to be, even if they are not being used. If this puzzles you, be aware that many apps (or parts of them) run unseen in the background. So, the more software you install, inevitably the more of these background apps there will be. Not only do they slow system performance, but they also affect shutdown and startup speeds. Examine the number of apps installed on the Start menu. Alternatively, go to **Programs** in the **Control Panel**.

Malware
Malware is a term that encompasses invasive software, such as adware, spyware, and browser hijackers. Apart from compromising your PC's security and intruding on your privacy, they can also slow your internet activities considerably and, in the case of hijackers, can have a real impact on the PC's performance.

The **Windows Security** utility is the Windows 11 answer to this problem and is enabled by default. In theory, this application should keep your system clean of all viruses and malware. In practice, however, it may not do so. Just as email spammers are constantly devising new ways to circumvent spam filters and other safeguards, the authors of viruses/malware are doing the same with antivirus software.

You have two ways to approach this problem: prevention or cure. To prevent malware from getting onto your PC, avoid:

● Downloading anything from the internet unless you are quite sure about the source.

● Browsing the internet with any of your web browser's security features turned off.

● Installing software from unverifiable sources.

If you must do any of the above, or already have, scan your system with antivirus and anti-malware apps.

Since the Control Panel is a legacy feature in Windows 11, it sometimes uses the terminology "programs" rather than "apps".

No anti-malware app is perfect, so to ensure your system is as clean as possible, it is a good idea to use two.

47

The **Spybot Search & Destroy** anti-malware app is available for free at safer-networking.org

The **Malwarebytes** anti-malware app is available for free at malwarebytes.org

System Restore

Windows 11 takes snapshots of the system files before any software updates are applied, or in any event once every seven days. You can also create a snapshot manually. The snapshots are known as **Restore Points** and are managed by **System Restore**.

Hot tip

System Restore returns system files to an earlier point in time, allowing you to undo system changes without affecting your documents, email, and other data files.

48

1   In **Settings**, access **System > About** and click on the **Advanced system settings** link

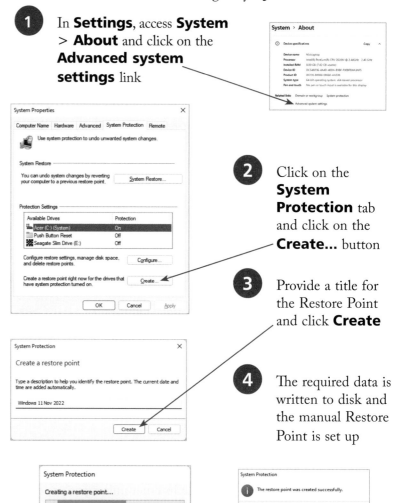

2   Click on the **System Protection** tab and click on the **Create...** button

3   Provide a title for the Restore Point and click **Create**

4   The required data is written to disk and the manual Restore Point is set up

Using Restore Points

The installation of a new app or driver software may make Windows 11 behave unpredictably or have other unexpected results. Usually, uninstalling the app or rolling back the driver will correct the situation. If this does not fix the problem, use an automatic or manual Restore Point to reset your system to an earlier date when everything worked correctly.

1 Select **System Protection** and click the **System Restore...** button

2 By default, this will offer to undo the most recent change. This may fix the problem

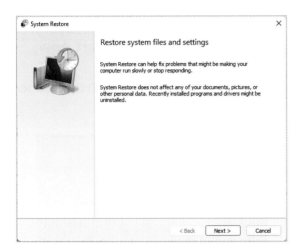

You can also run **System Restore from Safe Mode**, the troubleshooting option. Start up the computer and press **F8** repeatedly as your computer reboots, to display the boot menu, then select **Safe Mode**.

3 Otherwise, click a suitable item to use as the Restore Point

If the selected Restore Point does not resolve the problem, you can try again, selecting another Restore Point.

4 Follow the prompts to restart the system using system files from the selected date and time

PC recovery options

Windows 11 is a very stable and reliable operating system. However, it will inevitably go wrong on occasion and so users need to be aware of steps they can take to resolve any issues they experience.

If the problem is not too serious and the user can still get into Windows, the procedure is as follows:

1 Go to **Settings** > **System** > **Recovery**. Under **Advanced startup**, click **Restart now**

2 When the system restarts, choose **Troubleshoot** to see the following screen:

3 Click **Advanced options** to see a list of other troubleshooting options

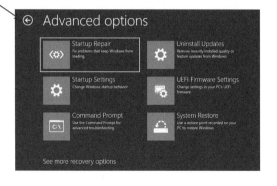

You can safely explore the **Advanced startup** options described here, then press the on-screen **Back** button to return to the first screen and choose **Continue**, to exit to Windows as normal.

If your PC simply will not boot up properly, try the **Startup Repair** option before anything else – it may well fix the problem.

System Image Recovery is similar to System Restore in that it restores the PC from an image file to a previous state, but unlike System Restore it destroys all the user's data. Accordingly, it is a "last resort" option to be used only when all others have failed. This is accessed from **See more recovery options** in the **Advanced options** window in Step 3 on the previous page.

Startup Repair attempts to resolve issues that are preventing the PC from starting. So if your PC won't boot up, this is the option to try first. See **Startup Settings** below.

Command Prompt is for advanced users only. It appears before Windows loads and can be used to enter commands to diagnose, check components, and for other recovery options.

Startup Settings provides a list of further troubleshooting options, such as **Safe Mode**, **Low-Resolution Video Mode**, **Boot Logging**, and more.

If the problem is so serious that you cannot get Windows running at all, you will have to access the recovery options a different way.

If you have a Windows 11 installation disk, the recovery options will be available from this. To do this, place the installation disk in the drive, and then boot the PC. When the **Install now** screen opens, you will see a **Repair your computer** option at the bottom. Click this and the recovery options will open. If you don't have an installation disk – as many PCs these days are sold without one – you will have to create a recovery disk. Windows provides you with an option to do this. However, you need to do it while your PC is functional – it's no good waiting until it has failed. You can do it by going to the **Control Panel (View by: Large icons/Small icons)** and clicking **Recovery**. Select the first option, **Create a recovery drive**, and simply follow the prompts. Note that you will need a USB drive for this.

If you want to start your PC in **Safe Mode**, select **Startup Settings** then click the **Restart** button that appears and choose the **F4** key option.

If you don't have a Windows 11 installation disk, be sure to create a recovery drive – you might need it one day!

Virtually all problems that occur with Windows can be repaired.

Refreshing the PC

There comes a time in the life of any well-used computer when it will benefit hugely from a good clearout. Over time, files are created and deleted, apps are installed and uninstalled, the inevitable crashes occur, and users do things they shouldn't. A PC can become clogged up with redundant and useless data, long-forgotten files and apps, and broken shortcuts. Furthermore, essential system or app files may have gone missing or been corrupted. At best, this will be the cause of irritating little faults and problems, and at worst, a serious decrease in system performance or loss of functionality.

There is absolutely nothing that can be done about this, no matter how carefully you maintain the PC. Traditionally, the only effective solution to this problem was a clean install; i.e. backing up all the data on the PC, reformatting the hard drive (which wipes the drive clean), installing a new copy of Windows, and then reinstalling the backed-up data and apps.

It is a procedure that returns the PC to an "as new" condition but does require a level of technical expertise that most users simply don't have. However, Windows 11 includes a **Reset this PC** utility that can be used to refresh your PC's operating system or to completely renew the state of your entire PC. Here, we look at how to refresh your PC to rejuvenate the operating system.

1 Access **Start** > **Settings** > **System**

2 Click the **Recovery** option

Recovery
Reset, advanced startup, go back

It is almost always easier to simply revert the system to a state prior to a fault manifesting itself than it is to isolate and repair the fault.

3 Click the **Reset PC** button in the **Recovery options** section

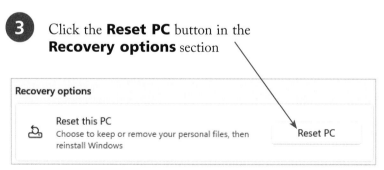

Recovery options

Reset this PC
Choose to keep or remove your personal files, then reinstall Windows

Reset PC

4 You are then presented with these two options:

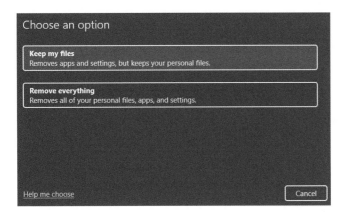

The **Keep my files** option allows you to refresh your PC. This is what will happen if you run the utility using that option:

- Your files and personalization settings won't change – this means that your data will not be deleted, and any changes you have made to the default personalization settings will be retained. The former is the big plus here, as it means you do not have to make a backup of your data and then reinstall it afterward.

- The PC's settings will be changed back to their defaults – this means that Windows 11 will be deleted and replaced by a new copy. Any configuration changes made to Windows settings will be lost.

- Apps from the Microsoft Store will be kept – apps installed from the Microsoft Store will not be deleted.

- Apps you installed from discs or websites will be removed – all third-party software will be deleted.

Effectively, then, the **Reset this PC** utility will install a new copy of Windows 11 while retaining the user's data and personalization settings. Everything else will be deleted. The big drawback is that users will probably have to reinstall/reconfigure most of their software, and reconfigure various Windows settings.

A big advantage of the **Reset this PC** utility is speed. It can reinstall Windows 11 in a fraction of the time taken by the original installer process.

The system refresh only replaces Windows 11 system files and settings.

The big drawback of the **Reset this PC** utility is that users will probably have to reinstall/reconfigure most of their software, and reconfigure various Windows settings.

Troubleshooting

On any computing system there are always things that go wrong or do not work properly. Windows 11 is no different, but there are comprehensive troubleshooting options for trying to address a range of problems. To use these:

1 Open the **Settings** app, select **System** and click the **Troubleshoot** option

2 Recommended troubleshooting options are displayed within the main window

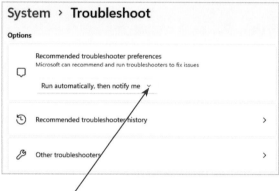

Recommended troubleshooter preferences includes a range of options that are selected automatically by Windows 11.

3 Click here to select options for how the recommended troubleshooters work

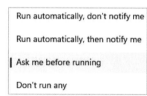

4 Click **Recommended troubleshooter history** in Step 2 to view the most recent troubleshooters that have been run

5 Click the **Other troubleshooters** button in Step 2 on the previous page to view troubleshooting options for specific hardware items and apps

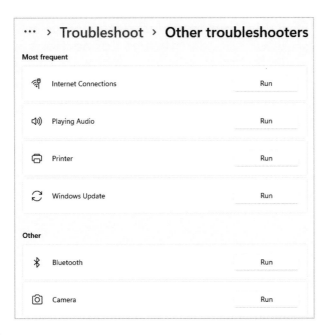

Try the troubleshooting options first for hardware devices before you try to physically repair any problems.

6 Click one of the categories to select it, and click on the **Run** button

7 The troubleshooting will run for the selected item and a report will be displayed once the troubleshooting has been completed. Click the **Close** button

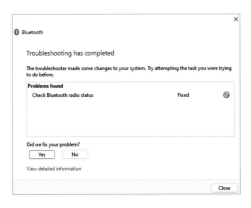

...cont'd

Network troubleshooting

One of the most common types of computing problems are those related to connections to the internet. Thankfully, there is a troubleshooting option specifically for this.

1 From the **Other troubleshooters** option in Step 5 on page 55, click the **Internet Connections** option

2 Click the option that most closely matches your network problem

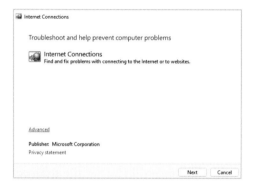

3 Most options have additional selections that can be made to try to solve the problem. Click these as required

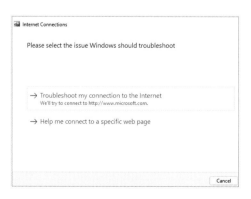

3 Startup and shutdown

Don't you just hate it when your PC insists on taking its own sweet time to start up and shut down? The procedures in this chapter will teach it some manners and ensure that its laggardly ways are a thing of the past.

Quick boot

When a computer is booted up, the BIOS (Basic Input/Output System) chip on the motherboard checks and initializes the system's hardware. It then searches all the drives (hard drive, CD/DVD drive, USB drives, etc.) for the operating system.

This tip ensures that it goes immediately to the drive on which the operating system is loaded – i.e. the hard drive – thus saving time:

1 Start the PC, and when you see text on the screen, press the key needed to enter the BIOS setup app (see the Hot tip to the left)

2 Using the arrow keys, open the **Advanced BIOS Features** page and press **Enter**

The key to enter the BIOS setup app is shown on the boot screen. With an AWARD BIOS it is usually **Delete**, and with an AMI BIOS it is usually **F2**. If you are unsure, try holding down one or more keys to cause a stuck key error – you may then be offered the option to continue boot or enter the BIOS setup app.

```
        Phoenix - AwardBIOS CMOS Setup Utility

Virus Warning                 [Disabled]
CPU Internal Cache            [Enabled]      Item Help
External Cache                [Enabled]
CPU L2 Cache ECC Checking     [Enabled]
Processor Number Feature      [Enabled]     Select Your Boot
Quick Power On Self Test      [Disabled]    Device Priority
First Boot Device             [HDD-0]
Second Boot Device            [CDROM]
Third Boot Device             [Floppy]
Boot Other Device             [Enabled]
Swap Floppy Drive             [Disabled]
Boot Up NumLock Status        [On]
Gate A20 Option               [Fast]
Ata 66/100 IDE Cable Msg.     [Enabled]
Typematic Rate Setting        [Disabled]
Security Option               [Setup]
OS Select For DRAM > 64MB     [Non-OS2]

Esc : Quit
F10 : Save & Exit Setup

        Virus Protection, Boot Sequence...
```

3 Scroll to **First Boot Device** and use the **Page Up/ Page Down** keys to cycle through the options and select **HDD-0**. Note that this only applies if you have just one drive in your PC – if you have more, you will need to choose the one Windows is installed on

The description and steps above relate to an AWARD BIOS. Users with a BIOS from other manufacturers will find that the terminology used, and page layouts, will differ.

BIOS speed boost

Every BIOS has a diagnostic utility called the Power On Self Test (POST), which checks that vital parts of the system, such as the video and memory, are functioning correctly. If there is a problem, it will warn the user accordingly in the form of a series of coded beeps (beep codes) or an error message.

However, the BIOS can be configured to skip through certain non-essential parts of the POST, thus speeding up boot time considerably.

1 In the BIOS setup app, open the **Advanced BIOS Features** page

```
           Phoenix - AwardBIOS CMOS Setup Utility

Virus Warning               [Disabled]
CPU Internal Cache          [Enabled]       Item Help
External Cache              [Enabled]
CPU L2 Cache ECC Checking   [Enabled]
Processor Number Feature    [Enabled]     Select your Boot
Quick Power On Self Test    [Enabled]     Device Priority
First Boot Device           [HDD-0]
Second Boot Device          [CDROM]
Third Boot Device           [Floppy]
Boot Other Device           [Enabled]
Swap Floppy Drive           [Disabled]
Boot Up NumLock Status      [On]
Gate A20 Option             [Fast]
Ata 66/100 IDE Cable Msg.   [Enabled]
Typematic Rate Setting      [Disabled]
Security Option             [Setup]
OS Select For DRAM > 64MB   [Non-OS2]

Esc : Quit
F10 : Save & Exit Setup

           Virus Protection, Boot Sequence...
```

2 Scroll to **Quick Power On Self Test** and select **Enabled**

3 Save your change then exit the BIOS setup app

Among other things, this will make the BIOS skip the memory test that occurs when you turn on your PC. It's a very basic test and the chances are, if you really do have bad memory, the test won't catch it anyway.

Note that some BIOSs have **Quick Power On Self Test** enabled by default. Not all do, though, so check it out.

Hot tip

Beep codes vary but an AWARD BIOS includes:

- **Repeating mid-tone**
  Memory error – check for missing or improperly-seated memory.

- **Repeating alternate high-tone/low-tone**
  CPU error– check for a damaged, overheated, or improperly-seated CPU.

- **Beep 1 long, 2 short**
  Video adapter error – check for an improperly-seated video card or disconnected monitor.

59

Hot tip

This setting has various names depending on the BIOS manufacturer. Examples are: **Perform Quick Memory Test, Quick Boot**, and **Quick Power On Self Test**.

Disabling unused hardware

Every time a computer is switched on, its hardware has to be detected and initialized by the BIOS. Thus, the more devices there are, the longer the PC takes to boot up.

While most of the PC's hardware is essential for it to run, in virtually all systems there are some devices that are not used. By disabling these, you can increase the PC's boot speed.

Beware

Don't disable hardware devices in the **Display adapters** and **System devices** categories – these are critical to the operation of your PC.

 1 Right-click the **Start** button and click **Device Manager**. Here, you will see a list of all the hardware installed on your system

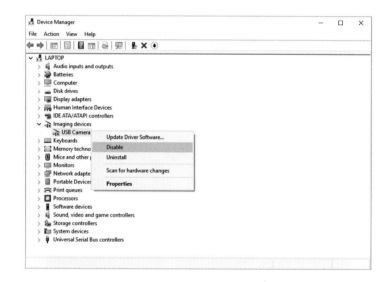

Hot tip

The webcam device can be disabled, as shown here – unless it is required for video calling or facial recognition, etc.

2 Go through the list by expanding categories. Disable any devices you do not use by right-clicking the device and clicking **Disable** on the context menu that appears

Examples of devices that are typically unused include:

● **Network adapters** – Most motherboards provide an integrated network adapter.

Hot tip

You may also find unused hardware that can be disabled in the BIOS.

● **Bluetooth controllers** – If you don't use Bluetooth you don't need to have it enabled.

● **Multimedia devices** – Integrated video and sound. Many users have dedicated video and sound cards so don't need these.

Streamlining the Fonts folder

Windows comes with a large number of fonts, all of which are installed in the **Fonts** folder. As each of these fonts is loaded when the PC starts up, the more there are, the longer startup takes to complete. Therefore, you can increase your boot speed by deleting all but the ones used by the system, and the ones you are likely to use.

1 Open the **Windows** folder on the **C:** drive and locate the **Fonts** folder. Right-click it, select **Copy** and save it in a backup location

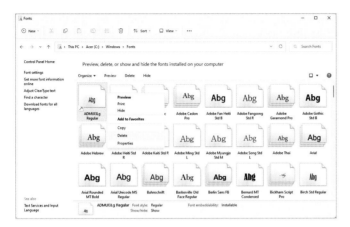

A font manager can be very useful for users who access the fonts on their systems regularly.

You can download the free **NexusFont** font manager at xiles.app

2 Now, open the original folder and simply work through the fonts, deleting any that are surplus to requirements; this should be the vast majority of them

Note that when you delete a font, a confirmation window appears warning that some text may not appear as intended if you delete the font. Click **Yes** to confirm the deletion of the font.

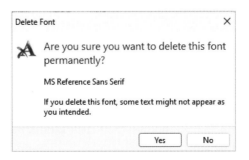

Be wary of downloading free fonts from the internet. These are often corrupt and may cause your system to lock up completely.

Should you subsequently find a need for any of the deleted fonts, just copy them back to the **Fonts** folder from your backup folder.

Clearing out the Startup folder

The next thing to look at is your startup apps. These are applications that open automatically when Windows starts, and are located in the **Startup** folder. Shortcuts to apps can be placed here by the user to automatically start them with Windows so that they are ready for immediate use. Also, some apps will place a link here automatically when they are installed.

Hot tip

The user's Startup folder is located at **C:\Users\ username\AppData\ Roaming\Microsoft\ Windows\StartMenu\ Programs\Startup**. To ensure the **AppData** folder is visible, hidden files, folders and drives have to be made visible in File Explorer, as shown on page 75.

As each of these apps must be loaded before Windows is ready for use, the more items there are in the **Startup** folder, the longer it will take to start Windows.

Check it out as follows:

1 Right-click the Taskbar and click **Task Manager** on the context menu to open that utility

2 Click the **Startup apps** tab in the left-hand sidebar. You'll see a list of applications that start with Windows, as shown below:

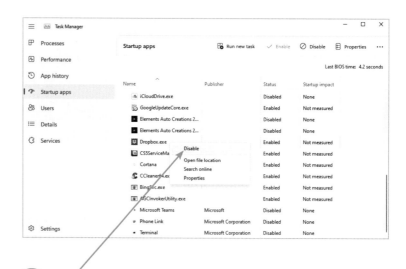

Beware

The more apps you have in your **Startup** folder, the longer the PC will take to boot.

3 Right-click apps you don't need to automatically start with Windows, then click **Disable** from the context menu

However, if there is something you'd rather keep, check the **Startup impact** column to see the impact it has on the PC's startup speed. If it says **Low** there is really no need to disable it, as its effect will be minimal.

Screen savers and wallpaper

In days gone by, computer monitors were prone to having an impression burnt into the screen by prolonged exposure to a static image. To guard against this unfortunate tendency, screen savers were invented. Apart from serving a useful purpose, they could also be fun. These days, however, that's all they are – fun. They are now completely superfluous in the modern computer system, as monitors are no longer susceptible to damage caused by static images.

Because a screen saver is actually an app, having one enabled means that Windows has one more application to load before it is ready to use. So, reduce your PC's startup time by disabling any screen saver that is currently active.

1 Open the **Settings** app and type **screen saver** into the **Search** box and click **Change screen saver**. In the **Screen Saver** settings, click in the **Screen saver** box and choose **(None)** from the drop-down box

With regard to wallpaper, these are large image files that have no function other than to make your desktop look cool. As with screen savers, they slow down the startup procedure as they also have to be loaded by Windows. Your best option here is to use a solid color as the background.

1 Open **Settings** > **Personalize**, then select **Background** and choose **Solid color** from the **Personalize your background** drop-down box

Beware

3D screen savers available on the internet can take a long time to load, may contain bugs, and can cause system instability.

63

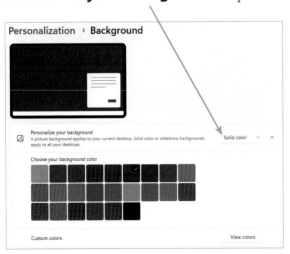

Shutdown issues can be difficult problems to identify. Device drivers are the most likely cause and this is what you should investigate first.

You can open **Device Manager** from the Power User menu to look for possible device-driver problems.

The **Event Log** will also highlight issues that are causing your PC to boot more slowly than it should.

Shutdown issues

When a Windows PC takes an unusually long time to shut down, the cause is almost always one of the following:

● A service or running process that is slow to close.

● The unloading of user-profile files.

● A non-responding application.

● A corrupted or incompatible device driver.

The first three in the list above have, to a certain degree, been addressed in recent versions of Windows, and therefore do not cause as many problems as they did with earlier versions. That said, on occasion they are still the cause of shutdown issues.

Device drivers are beyond Windows' control, as the decision to install a device driver is made by the user. Windows will warn if a driver being installed is potentially problematic but it cannot stop the installation. This is one of the biggest causes of Windows shutdown problems.

When in this situation, go to **Windows Tools > Component Services**. On the left, go to **Event Viewer (Local) > Applications and Services Logs > Microsoft > Windows > Diagnostics-Performance > Operational**.

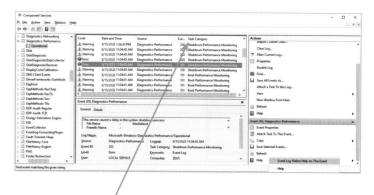

Look under **Task Category** for issues relating to **Shutdown Performance Monitoring**. Clicking an entry will reveal details of the application that is causing a delay in the shutdown process. Click the **Event Log Online Help** link to visit a Microsoft website for more detailed information.

Killing services quickly

When a PC's **Shut down** button is pressed, Windows closes all open applications, including any services that may be running. The length of time Windows allocates for the latter is set by the **WaitToKillServiceTimeout** Registry key – the default setting of which is 5,000 ms (5 seconds).

If all running services stop within 5 seconds, the PC shuts down. However, if they don't, the user is presented with a dialog box that offers two options: wait for the service to stop of its own accord, or force it to close. By lowering the default value, you can force tardy services to close more quickly and thus prevent them from slowing down the shutdown procedure.

Alternatively, use **Edit > Find** in the Registry Editor to locate the **WaitToKillServiceTimeout** Registry key.

1. Press **WinKey + R** and type **regedit** in the **Run** box, then press **Enter** and agree the UAC dialog

2. When the **Registry Editor** opens, navigate to **HKEY_LOCAL_MACHINE/SYSTEM/ CurrentControlSet**

3. Expand this item and click the **Control** folder on the left – on the right you will then see the **WaitToKillServiceTimeout** key

Services do need some time to close. The objective here is simply to speed up the process a little.

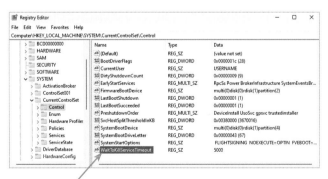

4. Double-click the key, and in the **Edit String** dialog box that opens, enter a lower value, then click **OK**

Resist the temptation to set too low a value in the **Edit String** dialog box, as this may lead to loss of data.

Putting the PC to sleep

Windows provides an option for closing down your machine known as **Sleep**. This is accessible from **Start** > **Power** > **Sleep**, or by pressing **Ctrl** + **Alt** + **Del** and clicking the **Power** button, or by clicking the **Power** button on the **Sign-in** screen, or by right-clicking on the **Start** button and selecting **Shut down or sign out** > **Sleep**.

On laptops, **Sleep** mode only saves an image to the memory – not to the hard drive as well.

File Explorer	Sign out
Search	Sleep
Run	Shut down
Shut down or sign out ⟩	Restart

Sleep mode is basically a combination of the old **Standby** mode and **Hibernate** mode.

In the old **Hibernate** mode, an image of the system was created on the hard drive and then the PC was powered off. The problem was that, in practice, it was not much quicker than just switching it off and then back on as normal.

Sleep mode monitors the laptop battery and intelligently transfers the image stored in memory to the hard drive when power runs low.

In the old **Standby** mode, an image of the system was created in memory and power was maintained only to essential devices such as the CPU. The problem here was that an application could override **Standby** and keep the PC running. Also, if power to the PC was lost for some reason, all unsaved data was lost.

Windows' **Sleep** mode saves all data in use to both the memory and the hard drive before cutting power to all but a few key components. The procedure takes just a few seconds. When a key is pressed, the mouse moved or the screen tapped, the system is restored from the image stored in the memory. If the machine has been powered off, the system is restored from the image stored on the hard drive on restart. Thus, there is no danger of data loss. Furthermore – and this is the major advantage of **Sleep** – it is quick, taking a few seconds to bring the PC back to life.

Use **Sleep** mode instead of **Shut down** to have your PC ready for work almost instantly at your next session.

Sleep mode eliminates the need to switch off a computer between sessions. Simply put the machine to sleep at the end of the day, and then have it up and running within a few seconds the following morning with a single keystroke or mouse click.

4 Productivity

Computers can be used for both entertainment and work. In this chapter the focus is on the latter, looking at ways to increase the efficiency with which you use your Windows 11 computer. These will help you to save time and also be more productive. The chapter also has some productivity tips, such as using Snap Layouts for multitasking.

Finding it fast

An important part of working efficiently and productively is being able to locate things quickly when needed. The worker who can lay their hands on the right tool when needed will get the job done faster than the one who has to go looking for it.

Working on a PC is much the same, so to make life easier for users in this respect, Windows 11 provides a **Search** utility. This is tightly integrated in the operating system and thus instantly accessible from virtually any location. You will find it in any File Explorer folder and through the Taskbar Search box. One of its best features is that it is contextual – i.e. its search is based on the user's current activity, whether it's searching for utilities in the Control Panel or for files and applications on the hard drive.

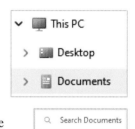

Folder searches

If you already know in which folder the file is located, select the location in File Explorer then use the Search box at the top-right of the folder; e.g. **Documents**. By default, the search will be conducted across the selected folder, as indicated in the Search box. Use **This PC** when you have no idea where to look.

Once you have undertaken a search, by entering a keyword in the Search box, the results are displayed in the main File Explorer window.

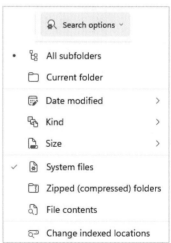

To refine the search, click the **Search options** button that is now on the File Explorer menu bar and select one of the available options.

Also available are filters, which help to speed up the search – these appear on the **Sort** button on the File Explorer menu bar and enable you to search by various criteria, such as **Date modified**, **Kind**, **Size**, etc.

By default, a folder search will only find content that is located in the folder in which the search is conducted.

Windows 11 Search

The **Search** function is also available from the Windows 11 Taskbar **Search** icon. Click on it to access the **Search** box and begin typing your query.

The search results produce a **Best match** suggestion and further **Apps**, **Documents**, and **Settings** category options. Select an item to view that result, or select any category heading to refine your results. Click the **More** button at the right-hand side of the top toolbar to access more search categories.

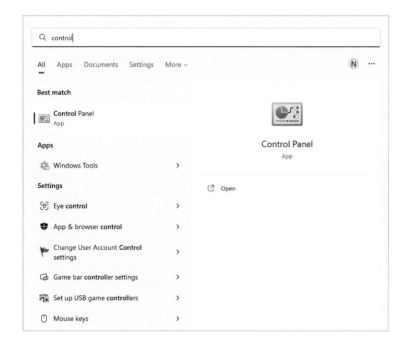

The **Cortana** personal digital assistant also lets you search using voice commands (access its app from the **All apps** section of the Start menu). The **Search** box and **Cortana** both conduct their searches using the Microsoft Bing search engine. However, **Cortana** voice search results are typically displayed in the Microsoft Edge web browser. For example, **find Ferrari** displays a web page listing search results. Voice searches within Windows 11 need to be phrased well to produce the best results. For filenames beginning with the term **Ferrari** try searching with the phrase **find my Ferrari documents** or **find my Ferrari pictures**.

Hot tip

You can find and open apps using the Taskbar **Search** icon – enter **notepad** then click the **Best match** result to open the **Notepad** app.

Hot tip

You can also open apps using the **Cortana** personal digital assistant – say **Hey Cortana, Open Notepad** if you have set this up in **Settings**.

Hot tip

If **Cortana** is not working or enabled in your country, select the required region and language (they have to be the same) in **Settings** > **Time & language** > **Language & region**.

69

Using search aids

Windows 11 provides two very useful tools that enable the user to increase the efficiency with which the **Search** utility is used.

File indexer

The first is the **Indexing** utility. When the operating system is run for the first time, it creates an index of all the files in the most commonly-used locations (note, not the entire computer). As a result, subsequent searches are much faster, as Windows searches the index rather than the computer.

Don't forget

Indexing proceeds in the background and may slow down during periods of user activity.

Don't forget

The Indexing options can be accessed by selecting **View by: Large icons/Small icons** in the main Control Panel window.

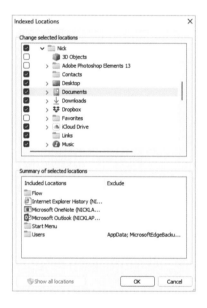

However, users who are in the habit of scattering files all over the place or adding storage devices to the PC – e.g. a second hard drive – can configure the utility to index any location they wish, or even the entire system.

To do this, go to **Control Panel > Indexing Options**. Click **Modify** to open the **Indexed Locations** dialog, then select locations to be included in the index.

Hot tip

Adding information to search filters about a file you're looking for will enable the file to be located more quickly.

To further refine indexing, go to **Control Panel > Indexing Options**, then click **Advanced** in the main **Indexing Options** window to open the **Advanced Options** dialog. Select the **Index Settings** tab or **File Types** tab, then choose your indexing preferences.

Beware

If you decide to index the entire computer, be aware that the procedure can take several hours. During this time, system performance may be adversely affected. This only needs to be done once, though.

File tagger

Tags provide a method of invisibly marking selected files. This makes the procedure of subsequently finding and organizing them much quicker and more efficient. Tagging is particularly useful on computers that have lots of images stored on them.

Use this feature as follows, in File Explorer:

Hot tip

You can add multiple tags to a picture. To separate tags, type a semicolon (**;**) between each tag.

 1 Open the folder containing the file to be tagged, then click **View** > **Show** > **Details pane** on the menu bar

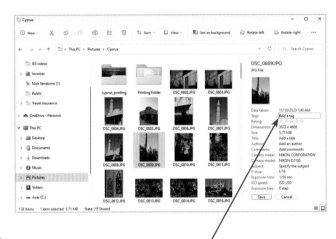

Hot tip

Add a star rating to rank your favorite media files – from one to five stars.

71

2 Select the file, click **Add a tag** and enter an appropriate word or phrase. Then, click **Save**

Another way to tag a file is to right-click it, select **Properties** and open the **Details** tab. Then, select **Tags** and press any key – this will open a text entry box alongside, as shown below:

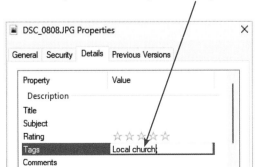

Type your tag name into the box. You can also add or change other properties in the same way – e.g. **Title**, **Comments**, etc. These all give you extra options when searching.

Don't forget

The **Tag** feature does not work with all file types. Microsoft file types – e.g. **.doc** or **.docx** (Word) – and some image files work but files from third-party apps don't.

Advanced searching

Searching in Windows 11 can be as simple as typing a few letters in the **Search** box. However, there are also advanced techniques that can be used, which can be helpful depending on where you're searching and what you're searching for.

Operators

One method of refining a search is to use the **AND**, **OR**, and **NOT** operators. These must be typed in capital letters. The table below shows how they work:

Operator	Example	Action
AND	library AND quick	Finds files that contain both of the words "library" and "quick"
NOT	library NOT quick	Finds files that contain the word "library" but not "quick"
OR	library OR quick	Finds files that contain either of the words "library" or "quick"

Depending on where you're searching, only certain search filters are available. For example, if you're searching the **Documents** library, you'll see different search filters than you would in the **Pictures** library.

You can use several filters in a search and also combine them with regular search terms to refine the search.

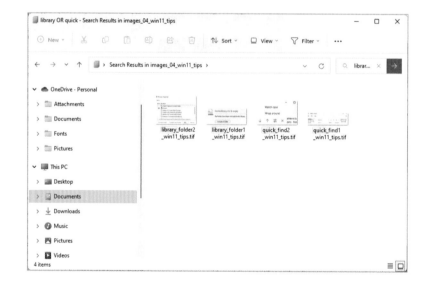

Keywords

If you cannot see the filter you need when you click in the **Search** box, try a keyword instead. This typically requires a property name to be specified, then a colon, sometimes an operator, and then a value. Some examples are shown below:

Example search term	Action
System.FileName:~<"report"	Finds files with names beginning with "report". ~< means "begins with"
System.FileName:="monthly report.doc"	Finds files named "monthly report.doc". = means "matches exactly"
System.FileName:~="pro"	Finds files with names containing the word "pro" or the characters "pro" as part of another word (such as "process" or "procedure"). ~= means "contains"
System.Kind:<>video	Finds files that aren't videos. <> means "is not"
System.DateModified: 09/24/2023	Finds files that were modified on that date. You can also type "System.DateModified:2023" to find files changed at any time during that year
System.Author:~!"john"	Finds files whose authors don't have "john" in their name. ~! means "doesn't contain"
System.Size:<1gb	Finds files less than 1GB in size
System.Size:>5gb	Finds files more than 5GB in size

You can also use the **AND, OR,** and **NOT** operators to combine search keywords.

Example search term	Action
System.Author:john AND dave	Finds files authored by John as well as files that include Dave
System.Author:john AND System.DateModified:>2023	Finds only files that are authored by John after 2023
System.Author:"john parker"	Finds files that are authored by John Parker
System.Author:(john* AND dave)	Finds files that have either John and Dave or Dave and John listed as authors

Hot tip

You can use a **?** wildcard for a single character ("rep?rt") and an asterisk ***** for multiple characters ("rep*").

Don't forget

System.FileName searches are case-sensitive, so "Report.doc" and "report.doc" are seen as different files.

Hot tip

In the final example on the left, note how adding parentheses can change the effect of a search term.

More right-click options

The right-click context menu offers many useful options. Let's see how to add some more options.

Move To folder... and Copy To folder...

The right-click **Cut** and **Copy** commands allow you to copy and move files to different locations. However, you have to go to the desired location to complete the operation. Here's a faster way:

A new **Copy To folder...** context menu option will let you easily create a duplicate file in your chosen location.

A new **Move To folder...** context menu option will let you easily relocate a selected file to your chosen location.

These string values are identical, except for **630** and **631** in the strings.

1 Open the Registry Editor by going to the Taskbar Search box and typing **regedit**. Then, locate the following key:
HKEY_CLASSES_ROOT\AllFilesystemObjects\ shellex\ContextMenuHandlers

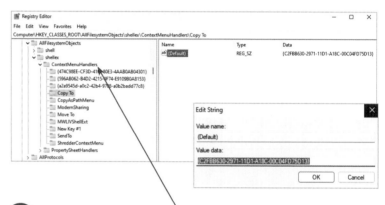

2 Right-click the **ContextMenuHandlers** folder and select **New > Key**. Name the key **Copy To**

3 Double-click the new key's **(Default)** icon in the right pane, to open its **Edit String** dialog, then precisely enter the following **Value data** string value:
{C2FBB630-2971-11D1-A18C-00C04FD75D13}

4 Repeat the above procedure, this time naming the key **Move To**, and precisely enter the following string value:
{C2FBB631-2971-11D1-A18C-00C04FD75D13}

5 Close the Registry Editor. Now, right-click a folder or file in File Explorer, click **Show more options**, and you will see new **Copy To folder...** and **Move To folder...** options

Adding options to the Send to menu

The **Send to** menu provides another very useful method of quickly relocating data. It can also be used to open a file with which an application is not associated. For example, if your PDF files open with the Acrobat app by default, you can use the **Send to** feature to open them with a different app.

If an application you would like to use in this way is not in the default **Send to** list, you can add it as described below:

1 In **File Explorer,** click the **See more** button on the menu bar. Select **Options** and click the **View** tab in the **Folder Options** panel. Check **On** the **Show hidden files, folders, and drives** option

2 Go to your **C:** drive, open the **Users** folder, and double-click your username. Then, select **AppData** > **Roaming** > **Microsoft** > **Windows** to now see the **Send to** folder

3 In the **Send to** folder, create shortcuts to the applications you want to add to the **Send to** menu – for example, to the **Microsoft Edge** app

4 When you have finished, close the folder and return to the desktop. Your applications will now be available from the **Send to** menu

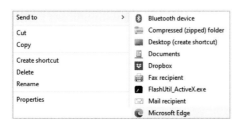

Hot tip

Quickly jump to the **Send to** folder by typing **%appdata%\ microsoft\windows\ sendto** into the **Run** box or File Explorer address bar.

Hot tip

Right-click on an app icon in File Explorer and choose **Open File Location** to help discover its path address on your system.

Beware

While the majority of apps work with the **Send to** feature, not all do. So, if you try this and the app doesn't appear in the **Send to** list, don't waste time trying to figure out why. Examples are apps from Microsoft 365/Office suites, such as Word, Excel and PowerPoint.

Quick file selection

The traditional way of selecting a bunch of files is to drag a box around them with the left mouse button depressed. Individual files are selected by holding down the **Ctrl** key.

Windows 11 provides a better way:

Hot tip

To deselect all checkbox-selected files in a folder, left-click once in an empty part of the folder.

1 Access **Folder Options** > **View** as shown on page 75

2 Scroll down the list and check the **Use check boxes to select items** option

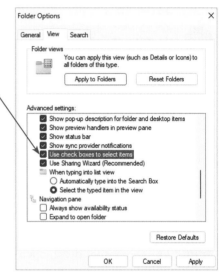

Hot tip

Checkboxes will appear beside each file in any **File Explorer** view – for any size icons, lists, details, tiles, or contents.

3 Now, click the **Apply** button to implement your change

The next time you open a folder, hovering the mouse over each file opens a checkbox to the left of the file. Simply check the box to select the file. This method is quicker and more precise.

Hot tip

You can still select files in the traditional way by dragging a box around the file icons.

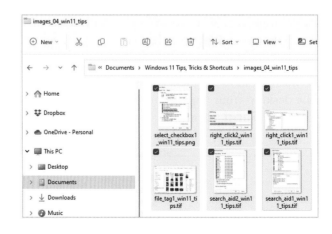

Batch renaming of files

Have you ever been in a situation in which you have a bunch of related files with an assortment of meaningless or unrelated names? To make order of them, you have to individually rename each file, which can be a tedious task.

Well, all that is now a thing of the past. Windows 11 provides you with a means of sequentially renaming any number of files with the minimum of effort.

1 Select the files to be renamed

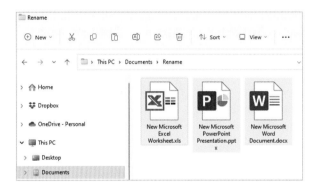

Hot tip

Click anywhere in the folder then press the **Ctrl** + **A** keyboard shortcut to quickly select all files.

2 Right-click the first file in the list and click the **Rename** icon. Type in a suitable name – for example, "AGM" – then click anywhere in the folder. The files will now all be automatically renamed, as shown below:

Don't forget

You can optionally use the Windows checkbox feature to select files; see the previous page.

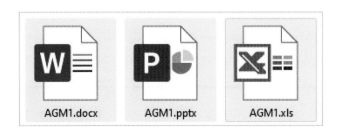

Hot tip

Notice that these automatically renamed files are named alike but are also sequentially numbered for like file types, such as **.docx**.

Changing/setting file associations

All files are designed to be opened with a specific type of app. For example, graphics files such as JPEG and GIF can only be opened by a graphics-editing app – e.g. **Paint** – or with an image viewer, such as Windows 11's **Photos** app.

A common problem that many users experience is when they install an app on their PC that automatically makes itself the default app for opening related files. If the user prefers the original app, they will have to reassociate the file type in question. Alternatively, the user might want to set a different app as the default.

Hot tip

You can open a file with an app not associated as its default by right-clicking the file and choosing from the **Open with** option.

1   Go to **Settings** > **Apps** > **Default apps**

2   Enter a file type in the Search box at the top of the window and click on the required app type for opening it

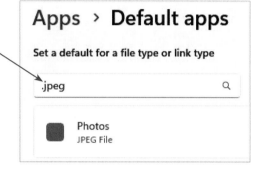

Apps > Default apps

Set a default for a file type or link type

.jpeg   🔍

Photos
JPEG File

Don't forget

If a newly-installed app has rudely hijacked your favorite files, you can re-associate those files with your favorite app.

3   You will now see a list of apps on the PC capable of opening the file. Use the app selected in Step 2, or select another one you want to associate with the file type – e.g. Paint

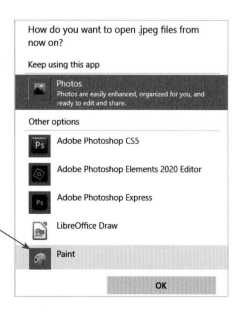

How do you want to open .jpeg files from now on?

Keep using this app

Photos
Photos are easily enhanced, organized for you, and ready to edit and share.

Other options

Ps   Adobe Photoshop CS5

  Adobe Photoshop Elements 2020 Editor

Ps   Adobe Photoshop Express

  LibreOffice Draw

  Paint

OK

Hot tip

Another way to associate apps is to right-click a file in File Explorer then choose **Properties** > **General** tab and click the **Change** button – select the app you want.

Closing non-responding apps

Every computer user has experienced this. You close an app but instead of disappearing gracefully and without fuss, it insists on hanging around. You click the red **X** button repeatedly but it refuses to go.

When this happens, after a few moments a dialog box will open asking if you want to wait until the app closes or whether you want to close it yourself. The latter option will usually do the trick; however, it doesn't always work.

In this situation, do the following:

1 Right-click the **Start** button and click **Task Manager**

2 Click the **Processes** tab and you will see the non-responding app. Right-click it and choose **End task**

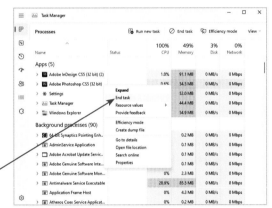

3 If this fails to work, right-click the app and choose **Go To Details**. Right-click it again and choose **End process tree**

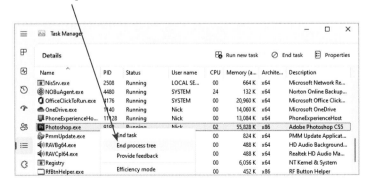

If you haven't already saved your data, closing a non-responding application with **Task Manager** may result in you losing that data.

If the desktop is unresponsive, just press **Ctrl** + **Alt** + **Delete** then select **Task Manager** to open the Task Manager dialog.

Every now and again, you will open a web page that causes your browser to stop responding. Use the tip in Step 3 to close it.

Customizing the Control Panel

The **Control Panel** is a very useful and often-overlooked section of Windows operating systems. From here, you can access settings that affect virtually all aspects of the computer.

It does, however, contain quite a few applications that will be of no interest to the average user – **Sync Center**, **Credential Manager**, and **Speech Recognition** are typical examples. There are others, though – such as **Internet Options**, **System**, and **Windows Tools** – that many people will use frequently.

This tip will give you quick access to the ones you use and allow you to forget about the ones you don't:

1 Create a new folder on the desktop and name it **Custom Control Panel**

2 Open the **Control Panel** (the real one) and create desktop shortcuts to the apps you use (right-click and select **Create Shortcut**)

3 Close the **Control Panel** and go back to the desktop. Now, drag the shortcuts to the **Custom Control Panel** folder

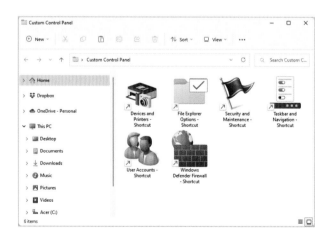

You now have a **Custom Control Panel** folder on the desktop that contains only the applications that you use. This lets you locate items quickly instead of having to search through a long list.

Hot tip

Look through the **Control Panel** utilities and you may find a lot of Windows features and settings that you didn't even know existed.

Hot tip

You cannot save shortcuts in the actual **Control Panel** – accept the dialog suggestion to save them on the desktop instead.

Don't forget

You can also use your new **Custom Control Panel** folder to create a space-saving custom toolbar on the Taskbar.

Organizing your data

Windows 11 includes a feature known as **Libraries**. This is a data management system that enables the user to quickly and easily organize specific types of data – e.g. images, documents, videos, etc.

The concept behind this is that of a single folder known as a "library", which contains user-defined sub-folders. The sub-folders are not actually stored in the library, though – they are still in their original locations. These could be a different hard drive, a flash drive, or even a separate PC (in the case of a networked system). However, they are all instantly accessible from the library folder. Furthermore, any changes to the contents of the sub-folders, wherever they may be, are dynamically updated in the library.

Windows typically starts you off with four default libraries – **Documents**, **Music**, **Pictures**, and **Videos**, which cover the main file types. These can be accessed on the Navigation pane of any **File Explorer** window by selecting **See more (...)** > **Options** from the menu bar, selecting the **View** tab, and checking **On** the **Show libraries** checkbox in the **Navigation pane** section. Should you wish to create a new library, you can do so by clicking on **Libraries** in the Navigation pane, then right-clicking in the content pane and selecting **Show more options** > **New** > **Library**.

To add content to a new library, open it and click the **Include a folder** button.

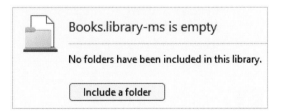

To add content to an existing library, right-click on the library and select **Properties**. Click on the **Add...** button and select a folder to be included in the library.

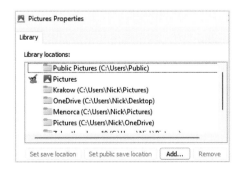

If you like things neat and tidy, or need to organize your data efficiently, Windows' **Libraries** feature is just what you need.

Windows indexes all library folders to enable fast searching.

See page 82 for more details about the Navigation pane.

Navigation pane folders

A very useful feature found in Windows **File Explorer** is the **Navigation pane** on the left-hand side of the window.

Hot tip

If the **Navigation pane** is not visible in File Explorer, click **View > Show > Navigation pane** on the menu bar to see it.

By default, the **Navigation pane** displays the commonly-accessed locations shown here on the right.

For those of you who wish to make the most of the **Navigation pane**, you may wish to see a more comprehensive selection of folders there.

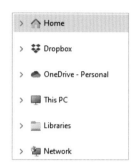

1 Open **File Explorer** in any folder and select the **See more (...)** button and then click the **Options** tab on the menu bar to open the **Folder Options** dialog, as shown on page 75

2 Select the **View** tab then scroll down to the **Navigation pane** section and check **Show all folders**

Hot tip

Click any folder in the **Navigation pane** and see the number of items contained in that folder displayed on the **File Explorer** status bar.

3 Click the **Apply** button to implement your changes, then **OK** to close the **Folder Options** dialog

4 Now, see that the **Navigation pane** contains a more comprehensive selection of folders – listed under the **Desktop** folder

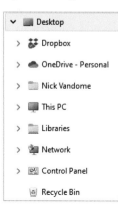

Snapping your apps

Universal Windows apps are designed to look great full-screen. However, with the large wide-screen monitors available today, many users will find it irritating to have their entire desktop real-estate taken up by just one program.

To address this issue, Windows 11 offers a feature called **Snap**, which enables users to run up to four apps side by side. The actual number depends on the monitor's resolution. Resolutions of 2,560 x 1,440 pixels can snap four apps. Resolutions less than this will only be able to snap two or three.

Here, two apps are snapped – File Explorer and the Settings app

To set this up:

1. Open the first app then click its window title bar and drag it out to the left edge of the screen. Release the mouse button to see the app window snap to the left half of the screen

2. Now, open the second app and drag it out to the right edge of the screen. Release the mouse button to see the app window snap to the right half of the screen

If the screen's resolution allows, you can repeat this with a third or fourth app, displaying one app in each corner. It's as easy as that.

One way in which this feature may prove to be useful is that it enables a Universal Windows app to be run alongside a traditional Windows app. For example, you can browse the web with **Microsoft Edge** and make notes alongside in **Notepad**.

The **Snap** functionality can be turned **On** or **Off** in **Settings** > **System** > **Multitasking**, where other settings for how this operates can also be applied.

For the Windows **Snap** feature to work, the device must have a screen width of at least 1,366 pixels. If you are having problems, check this out by going to **Settings** > **System** > **Display**.> **Display Resolution**.

Snap Layouts

An extension of the Snap functionality shown on page 83, known as **Snap Layouts**, provides great flexibility when it comes to working with windows: it is possible to display up to four active windows at a time, in a range of formats. **Snap Layouts** can be accessed from the control buttons at the top of any window. To use **Snap Layouts**:

1 Open an app and move the cursor over this button in the right-hand corner of the window. This displays the **Snap Layouts** panel

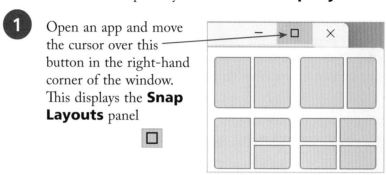

2 Click one of the thumbnails in the **Snap Layouts** panel

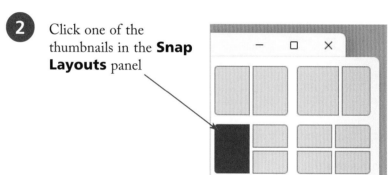

3 The app is displayed in the position selected in Step 2

Beware

Don't click on the button in Step 1 as this will maximize the window.

84

Beware

Not all third-party apps support the **Snap Layouts** feature.

4 If there are other open apps, they will be displayed as thumbnails in one of the available **Snap Layouts** panels. Click one of the thumbnails to maximize the selected app in the panel

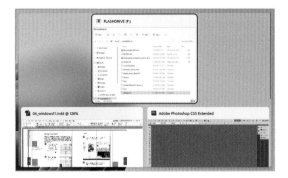

Apps can be rearranged once they have been assigned a position in a Snap Layout, by accessing the Snap Layout as in Step 1 on the previous page, and selecting a new location for the app.

5 Open another app and repeat the process in Steps 1 and 2 on the previous page to position it as required

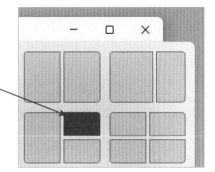

Apps can be "unsnapped" from their positions, by clicking and holding on the title bar and dragging them into a new position.

6 The app is displayed in the position selected in Step 5

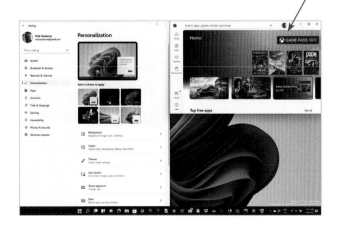

If you want to rename a file, rather than right-clicking it and choosing **Rename**, select it with the mouse then press the **F2** function key.

Have you ever needed to insert the date and time into a **Notepad** document? Here's an easy way – rather than typing it, just press the **F5** function key.

Miscellaneous tips

Switching to full-screen mode

When you're working in a folder that contains a large number of files, you can reduce the amount of scrolling necessary by simply pressing the **F11** function key. This switches the folder to full-screen view. Press **F11** again to revert to the normal view.

Accessing an inaccessible PC

When you're working in full-screen mode, both the desktop and Taskbar are hidden. Also, many games do the same by running permanently in full-screen mode.

If you need to open a file or app when in this situation, you can access the PC by pressing the Windows key (**WinKey**).

Whether in Desktop or Tablet mode, this opens the **Start** menu. Press **WinKey** again to close the **Start** menu.

Restoring previous folders at sign-in

If you sign off with a bunch of folders open, Windows closes them all for you. If you want the folders to reopen in their original size and position when you sign in again, do this:

1 Access the **File Explorer Options** > **View** tab as shown on page 75

2 Check the **Restore previous folder windows at logon** box

3 Click the **Apply** button to implement your choice, then click **OK**

4 Sign off then sign back in to see your open folders retained

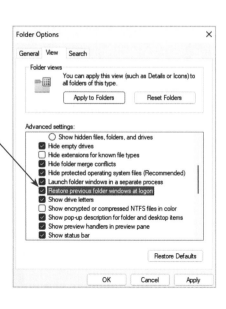

Bypassing the Recycle Bin

If you can live without the safety net of the **Recycle Bin**, you can speed up file deletion by doing away with it completely.

1 Right-click the **Recycle Bin** and click **Properties**

2 Select the **Don't move files to the Recycle Bin. Remove files immediately when deleted.** option, then click **Apply > OK**

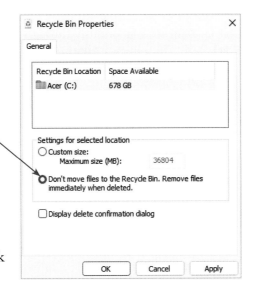

Recycle Bin Properties ✕

General

Recycle Bin Location	Space Available
Acer (C:)	678 GB

Settings for selected location
○ Custom size:
   Maximum size (MB):   36804
◉ Don't move files to the Recycle Bin. Remove files immediately when deleted.

☐ Display delete confirmation dialog

[OK] [Cancel] [Apply]

Hot tip

Another way to bypass the **Recycle Bin** is to hold down the **Shift** key as you click **Delete**.

Starting your favorite apps automatically

This tip will enable you to start any application automatically with Windows so that it is up and running when the desktop appears:

1 Press **WinKey + R**. In the **Run** box, type **C:\Users**_username_**\AppData\Roaming\Microsoft\ Windows\Start Menu\Apps\Startup** (where _username_ is the name of your profile folder)

2 The **Startup** folder will open – create shortcuts to the apps you want to auto-start. The next time you start the PC, the apps will launch automatically

Hot tip

Select the **Display delete confirmation dialog** option to guard against the accidental deletion of a file.

Quick zoom

If you want to zoom in on the contents of a folder, instead of using the **View** menu, hold down the **Ctrl** key and scroll the mouse wheel. Move forward to zoom in and backward to zoom out. This works in any Windows folder, on the desktop, in Microsoft Edge, and with most third-party applications.

Hot tip

When working in Windows, a quick way to undo your last action (provided you have not bypassed the **Recycle Bin**) is to press the **Ctrl + Z** keys. For example: if you have deleted a file by mistake, rather than opening the **Recycle Bin** and searching through it, pressing **Ctrl + Z** will restore the file instantly.

...cont'd

Quick searching

You've got a text document open and need to find a specific word, or all instances of one. The Windows **Search** utility isn't much use in this situation.

Rather than read laboriously through the document, just press **Ctrl** + **F**. This opens a **Find** utility that will go straight to the required word and highlight it for you.

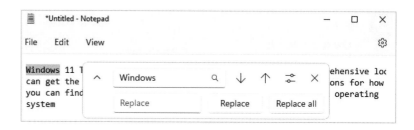

This works in any Windows text document, such as **Notepad**, **WordPad**, and **Journal**. It also works in most word-processor and desktop-publishing apps, all **Office** apps and on most web pages.

Copy as path

Here's a handy little feature that can be a real time saver. Now and again, you may need to find out the exact path of a file or folder. This could be to change a setting in the Registry, or to copy a link from a network file to share into an email or other destination.

The usual way to do this is to right-click the file and choose **Properties**. Next to **Location** in the **General** tab is the file's path you can copy and paste.

A quicker way is to right-click the file or folder while holding the **Shift** key down, and click **Copy as path**. Then, go to your destination, right-click, and choose **Paste**. Voilà! Job done.

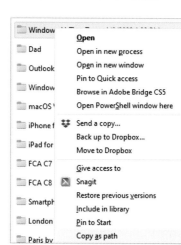

5 Things you can do without

This chapter shows you how to disable, but not remove, some of the features in Windows 11 that you do not always need and that can slow down performance.

User Account Control (UAC)

User Account Control (**UAC**) is a security feature designed to protect users from themselves; i.e. unwittingly making changes to the system that can compromise its security.

The most obvious manifestations of **UAC** are the **Do you want to allow...** dialog boxes that pop up when the user tries to do certain actions – installing an app, for example – and the **Secure Desktop** (when access to the desktop is removed).

These dialogs quickly become extremely tiresome, so getting rid of **UAC** (or reducing its level) is perhaps the first thing many users will want to do.

This is actually very simple, as we see below:

1 Go to **Control Panel** > **User Accounts** > **User Accounts**, then click **Change User Account Control settings**

2 Drag the slider to adjust the level of **UAC** (the bottom of the slider is off completely)

Beware

You should not disable **UAC** completely unless you are aware of the security issues involved. It is there for a reason.

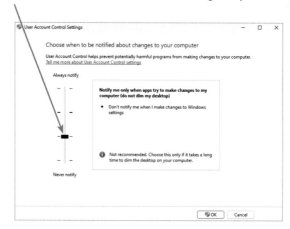

Notifications

Many people find the notifications that regularly spring up from the system tray notification area very irritating. Although they do sometimes give useful information, most of the time it is something obvious or that is already known to the user.

For those of you who can do without these notifications, the solution is as follows:

1 Access **Settings** > **System** > **Notifications**

2 Drag the **Notifications** button from **On** to **Off** to specify that you do not want to receive notifications

3 If **Notifications** is **On**, drag individual buttons **On** or **Off** to allow notifications for those items. Click on an item to view its notification options

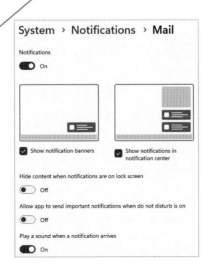

Notifications sometimes offer useful advice. For example, if your hard drive is running low on space, a notification will warn you.

The **Snap** feature simplifies the process of dragging and dropping between two windows, or comparing their content. With **Snap**, you can grab a window and move your mouse to the edge of the screen and the window will resize to fill half the screen. Repeat with the other window to have two side-by-side windows. See pages 83-85 if you do want to use the **Snap** feature and also **Snap Layouts**.

Without **Snap**, a considerable amount of mouse movement is needed to resize and position two windows side by side.

Snap

Windows 11 features a novel way to arrange your windows. This is known as **Snap** and it basically provides a quick way of resizing and tiling windows.

However, this is a feature that some users may want to disable, as at times it will cause you to resize a window when all you were intending to do was move it to a different part of the screen.

The **Snap** feature can be disabled as follows:

1 Go to **Settings** > **System** > **Multitasking**

2 If the **Snap windows** option is **On**, there will be additional checkboxes to determine its functionality

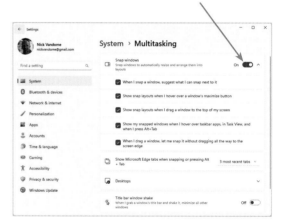

3 Turn **Off** the **Snap windows** option to disable it

Reporting problems

Every time an application experiences an error and is closed down by the system, the **Report Problems** utility will spring to life asking if you want to seek a solution from Microsoft. If you're the one in a million who will actually do this, then read no further. If you've no intention of complying, though, you'll want to get rid of this irritation as soon as possible.

Beware

Take care when editing the Windows Registry as it may compromise your system settings.

1 Go to **Control Panel** > **System and Security** > **Security and Maintenance**, then click on **Maintenance** to expand those settings – see that **Report problems** is turned **On**

2 Open the Windows Registry Editor (regedit) at **HKEY_LOCAL_MACHINE\SOFTWARE\Microsoft\ Windows\Windows Error Reporting**

Don't forget

Previous versions of Windows provided an option to turn **Off Report Problems**, but Windows 11 prefers you to leave it turned **On**.

3 Right-click in the right pane and choose **New** > **DWORD (32-bit) Value** and name the key **disabled**

4 Double-click this new key, then set its **Value data** to **1** and click **OK**

Don't forget

5 Now, re-open **Control Panel** > **Security and Maintenance** > **Maintenance** and see that the **Report problems** setting is turned **Off**

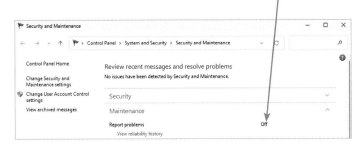

Before you disable **Report Problems**, you should be aware that, if it is available, Microsoft will send you the solution to the problem. So, while it is undoubtedly irritating, it can help prevent a repeat occurrence of the problem in the future.

AutoPlay

Windows 11 **AutoPlay** attempts to be helpful by providing related options that the user may not readily know how to access. Whenever removable media (DVDs, external hard drives, USB flash drives, etc.) are connected to the PC, a dialog box opens offering options that Windows thinks is relevant to the content on the media.

Many users, however, have no need for **AutoPlay** and find it is more of a nuisance than anything else. It can be disabled, or modified, as follows:

Hot tip

AutoPlay has long been regarded as an unsecure feature that provides an entry point for viruses. The version supplied with Windows 11 is much more secure.

1 Go to **Control Panel** > **AutoPlay**

2 To disable **AutoPlay** completely, uncheck the **Use AutoPlay for all media and devices** option

Don't forget

You can modify **AutoPlay** for different media by choosing from the drop-down menus.

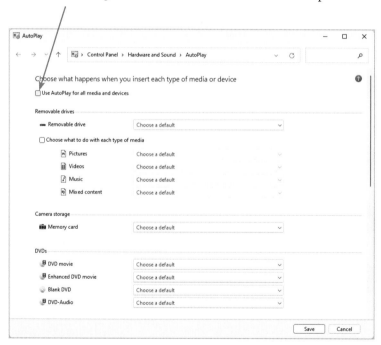

3 Click the **Save** button to implement the change, then insert some media to see **AutoPlay** now does not appear

OneDrive

The **OneDrive** cloud-based storage facility is heavily integrated into Windows 11, as Microsoft believes it is important to synchronize users' data and media across all their devices. By default, the **OneDrive** app is set to start when you sign in to Windows 11. This ensures that all the content within each folder you choose to sync on your PC is automatically kept in sync with your online **OneDrive** account.

Although **OneDrive** is regarded by many as a very useful facility, some users may not wish to use all of its features. Its setting can be managed as follows:

1 Go to the Taskbar **system tray** and right-click on the **OneDrive** icon

2 Click the **Settings** option to open the OneDrive settings

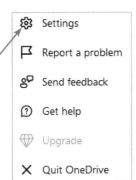

⚙ Settings

🏳 Report a problem

💬 Send feedback

⑦ Get help

◇ Upgrade

✕ Quit OneDrive

3 In the settings, click on the **Manage backup** button to specify which folders are backed up by OneDrive; e.g. you may just want to have your Documents and Pictures folders backed up in this way

Hot tip

If the **OneDrive** icon is hidden in the system tray, go to **Settings** > **Personalization** > **Taskbar** > **Other system tray icons** then slide **On** the **Microsoft OneDrive** toggle button.

Hot tip

If you choose not to start **OneDrive** automatically when you sign in to Windows, you can start it manually at any time by clicking **Start** > **All apps** > **OneDrive**.

Beware

Only set your PC to automatically sign in if you are absolutely the only user of the PC.

Sign-in password

By default, every time a Windows 11 PC is started, a password has to be entered before the Start screen opens. However, for the many users who don't require the security provided by password protection, not only is this a nuisance but it also slows down the startup procedure unnecessarily.

To get rid of the requirement to sign in:

1 Press **WinKey** + **R**, to open the **Run** box, then enter **netplwiz** – to open the **User Accounts** dialog box

2 Uncheck the **Users must enter a user name and password to use this computer** option

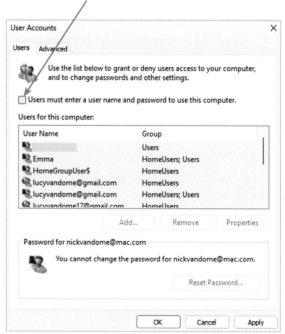

Beware

The password boxes cannot be left blank for this technique to work.

3 Click **Apply** to make the change

4 Select your user name and enter the current password (twice) – then click **OK**

5 Restart your PC to see that you no longer need to type in your password

6 Customization

This chapter details some of the ways to change the default appearance of Windows 11 so that you can personalize your PC.

The Windows interface

Customizing the look and feel of Windows 11 is a good way to make it feel like it is your own personal device. This can be done with some of the options in the **Personalization** section of the **Settings** app. This includes customizing the desktop background:

1 Open the **Settings** app and click on the **Personalization** tab

2 Click the **Background** option to select a new desktop background

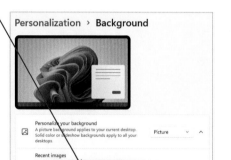

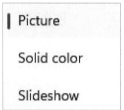

Click in the **Personalize your background** section in Step 2 and select an option for the background, from **Picture**, **Solid color** or **Slideshow**.

| Picture |
| Solid color |
| Slideshow |

3 The image selected in Step 2 becomes the desktop background

4 To select one of your own pictures for the desktop background, click the **Browse photos** button next to the **Choose a photo** option

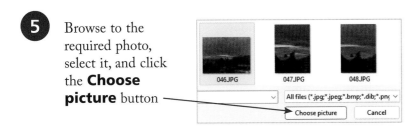

| Choose a photo | Browse photos |
| Choose a fit for your desktop image | Fill ⌄ |

5 Browse to the required photo, select it, and click the **Choose picture** button

6 The photo is added to the **Background** section of the **Personalization** settings, and remains available here even if another background is selected

Don't forget

Click in the **Choose a fit for your desktop image** box to specify how the picture fills the background screen. The options are: **Fill**, **Fit**, **Stretch**, **Tile**, **Center**, and **Span**.

7 The photo is added as the desktop background

...cont'd

Personalizing colors

Many of the color elements of Windows 11 can also be personalized. To do this:

1 Within the **Personalization** settings, click the **Colors** option

2 The color personalization options are displayed within the main **Colors** window

Hot tip

The **Light** and **Dark** mode options in Step 4 are applied to the Taskbar and the Start menu.

3 For the **Choose your mode** option, click here

4 Select an option for the colors for the Windows 11 interface, from **Light**, **Dark**, or **Custom**

5 The same color options as in Step 4 can also be selected for the **Choose your default Windows mode** and **Choose your default app mode** options

6 Drag the **Transparency effects** button **On** to enable the background behind a window to show through it to a certain degree

7 Turn the **Show accent color on Start and taskbar** and **Show accent color on title bars and windows borders** options **On** or **Off**, as required

Hot tip

If the **Transparency effects** button is **On**, the colors behind a window will change as the window is moved around the screen.

8 To select your own colors for accent colors, click on the **Accent color** section and select the **Manual** option

9 Click on the **View colors** button

10 Click on an area of the color chart to select a new color and click on the **Done** button

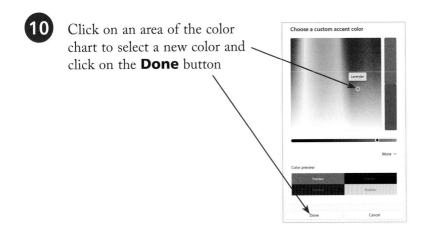

Using themes

Themes in Windows 11 can be used to customize several items for the look and feel of Windows.

1 Open **Settings** and click on the **Personalization** tab

2 Click the **Themes** option

3 The current theme is displayed

4 Make a selection for a customized theme, using **Background**, **Color**, **Sounds** and **Mouse cursor**

The preset themes in Step 5 combine all of the elements in Step 4 that can be used to customize a theme.

5 The selections for the customized theme are shown in the **Current theme** preview window

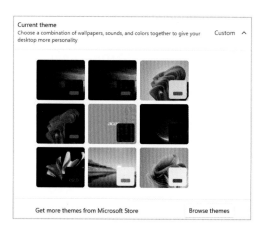

6 Click the **Save** button to use it for the current theme

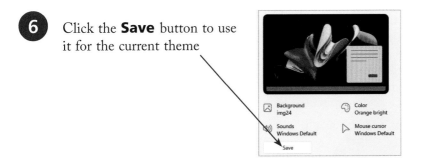

7 Click one of the preset themes to select it rather than customizing one

8 Elements of the preset theme are displayed in the preview window

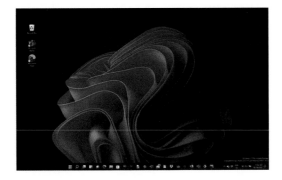

An internet connection is required to download more themes from the Microsoft Store.

9 Click on **Get more themes from Microsoft Store** to download more themes that can be used on your computer

Get more themes from Microsoft Store   Browse themes

The Taskbar

The Taskbar is a highly configurable part of Windows, and setting it up to suit your method of working is important. There are quite a few adjustments you can make here that are not obvious at first glance. By default, the Taskbar looks like this, displaying pinned and open apps, and the system tray at the right-hand side:

When more than one window in an app is open, this is displayed from the same icon on the Taskbar, by moving the mouse cursor over the app's icon:

To personalize the Taskbar:

1 Right-click on an empty area within it, click the Taskbar, and select the **Taskbar settings** button

2 The main Taskbar personalization categories are displayed. Click on each category to expand it and view its options

3 In the **Taskbar items** category, drag the buttons **On** or **Off** for **Search**, **Task View**, **Widgets** and **Chat**, as required, to show or hide them on the Taskbar, and the same for **System tray icons**

Hot tip

If you need as much screen space as possible, the **Automatically hide the taskbar** option in Step 4 can be a useful one, although in most cases this will probably not be required.

105

4 Click the **Taskbar behaviors** button to access more options for customizing the Taskbar, such as specifying its alignment, automatically hiding it, showing badges on icons when there are new notifications for the related app, and using the far right-hand corner of the Taskbar to display the desktop

Taskbar behaviors
Taskbar alignment, badging, automatically hide, and multiple displays

| Taskbar alignment | Center ∨ |

☐ Automatically hide the taskbar

☑ Show badges on taskbar apps

☑ Show flashing on taskbar apps

☐ Show my taskbar on all displays

☑ Show recent searches when I hover over the search icon

When using multiple displays, show my taskbar apps on — All taskbars ∨

☑ Share any window from my taskbar

☑ Select the far corner of the taskbar to show the desktop

Hot tip

If you can't find an icon that appeals, you can find thousands more available on the internet.

Don't forget

To associate downloaded icons with an app, in Step 3 use the **Browse...** button to find and select an icon.

System icons

Windows comes with a default set of system icons. These won't be to everyone's tastes though, so fortunately it's an easy task to change them to something more to your liking. To change the icon of a system folder, such as **This PC** or the **Recycle Bin**, you first have to create a shortcut to it. To demonstrate this, we will change the icon for the **Recycle Bin**:

1 Right-click the **Recycle Bin** icon and click **Show more options** > **Create shortcut** to create a shortcut on the desktop displaying the regular icon

2 Right-click the shortcut, click **Properties** > **Shortcut**, and then the **Change Icon...** button. This will open an icon folder

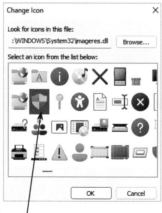

3 Select your preferred replacement icon and click **OK** to close the **Change Icon** dialog

4 Now, click **Apply** to implement the change, and click **OK** to close the properties dialog

Now, you can delete the original **Recycle Bin** icon. This procedure will work with most system folders. It will also work with third-party apps, most of which come with an icon folder of their own (these open instead of the icon folder shown above).

Folder icons

Apart from changing icons for system folders and third-party applications, Windows allows you to change (and also customize) individual folder icons.

Do this as follows:

1 Right-click inside the folder you want to customize and click **Show more options** > **Customize this folder**

2 To customize the folder with an image, select the **Customize** tab then click the **Choose File...** button

3 Browse to select a desired image, then click **Apply** > **OK** and it will be inserted into the folder icon (as below)

4 To change the folder's icon, click the **Change Icon...** button, then browse to an icon folder and choose an icon

If you place a folder customized in this way on the desktop, you may need to select a larger icon size to see the picture appear.

Using pictures is a useful way of personalizing folders, and also provides another method of readily identifying their contents.

Windows 11 Tips, Tricks & Shortcuts

Dialog box:

Windows 11 Tips, Tricks & Shortcuts Properties ✕

General | Sharing | Security | Previous Versions | Customize

What kind of folder do you want?
Optimize this folder for:

Documents ⌄

☐ Also apply this template to all subfolders

Folder pictures
Choose a file to show on this folder icon.

Choose File...

Restore Default

Folder icons
You can change the folder icon. If you change the icon, it will no longer show a preview of the folder's contents.

Change Icon...

OK | Cancel | Apply

Picture icons are an alternative way of identifying the contents of a folder.

You may need to select a larger icon size in order to see the image placed in a folder.

107

Click the **Restore Default** button on the **Customize** tab to stop using the inserted image on the folder.

Displaying a sign-in message

In certain situations it can be useful to greet users of a computer with a message when they sign in. This might be something friendly, or a warning of some description. An example of the latter could occur in an office environment where company email and internet facilities might be misused by employees.

1 Open the Registry Editor and locate the following key: **HKEY_LOCAL_MACHINE\SOFTWARE\Microsoft\ WindowsNT\CurrentVersion\Winlogon**

2 Double-click the **LegalNoticeCaption** key. In the **Value data** box, type your caption – e.g. **ATTENTION** – and click **OK**

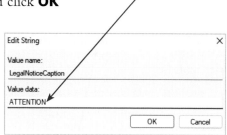

3 Now, click the **LegalNoticeText** key and type a message in the **Value Data** box

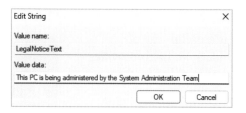

4 Click **OK**, restart the computer, and your message will be displayed before the **Sign-in** screen appears

7 Privacy

This chapter looks at privacy and security on your PC and the internet.

Hiding your browsing tracks

Browsing history

In the same way that Windows keeps records of user activity, so does the Microsoft Edge web browser.

This information is held in three categories:

- **Browsing history** – A chronological record of every website and page the user has visited.

- **Cookies and saved website data** – Cookies are text files that websites download to your PC. They have several purposes; one is to identify the user should they visit that website again. Often, the cookie data will also reveal the type of website – for example, **nick@luckydollarcasino**

- **Cached data and files** – A cache of the pages you have accessed. Should you revisit a particular web page, your browser will retrieve it from this cache rather than from the web. This makes access to the page quicker.

For users who wish to keep their internet activities private, Microsoft Edge provides a **Clear browsing data** utility.

Beware

Don't forget to check your internet **Favorites**. When accessed, certain websites will automatically place a link to their website here. Common culprits in this respect are porn and gambling websites. Anyone who happens to use your browser may see anything that has been added in this way.

1 Open Microsoft Edge, then click the **... (Settings and more)** button and then **Settings > Privacy, search, and services** in the left-hand sidebar

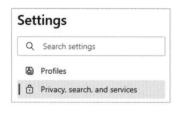

Settings

Q Search settings

▣ Profiles

🛡 Privacy, search, and services

Don't forget

The **Clear browsing data** utility lets you eradicate all records of your internet activities, or just some of them by checking certain items.

2 Under the **Clear browsing data** heading, click the **Choose what to clear** button

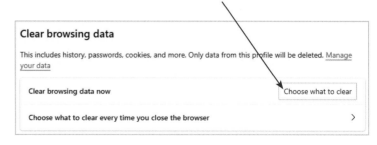

Clear browsing data

This includes history, passwords, cookies, and more. Only data from this profile will be deleted. Manage your data

Clear browsing data now   Choose what to clear

Choose what to clear every time you close the browser   >

3 Check the categories to be cleared, then click the **Clear now** button to implement your choice

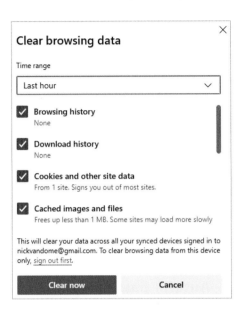

4 Click the **Choose what to clear every time you close the browser** button in Step 2 on the previous page. Drag the buttons **On** or **Off**, as required, to specify the items that you want cleared whenever you close the Edge browser

...cont'd

Autofill

Microsoft Edge has a feature called **Autofill** that enables the browser to automatically enter user names, passwords and data entered on web-based forms. This can be convenient as it saves the user from having to type out this information each time.

However, it can also be dangerous, as it allows other people to access your password-protected pages and see what data you've entered into forms, etc. It will also enable any snooper to see which websites you have visited, and any keywords entered in search engine Search boxes.

If you wish to keep this type of information private, then you need to disable **Autofill** or alter its settings

1 Go to **Settings** then click the **Profiles** tab in the left-hand sidebar

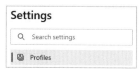

2 Drag the **Autofill passwords** button **On** or **Off** to activate or disable this as required

3 Click the **More settings** option to access further options for managing passwords and Autofill in the Edge browser

InPrivate browsing

As we have seen on pages 110-111, it is possible to delete your browsing history after each session. However, there are two problems with this approach:

● You may forget to do it.

● You have to delete the entire history when maybe all you want to do is to delete a small part of it – it's an all-or-nothing action.

The solution is a feature in Microsoft Edge called **InPrivate browsing**. When used, **InPrivate** temporarily suspends the browser's automatic caching functions and, at the same time, keeps your previous browsing history intact. A typical example of when you might want to do this is buying a gift online for a loved one – once done, you can revert to browsing as normal. Your browsing history up to the point of opening the **InPrivate** session is kept, but the **InPrivate** session itself is not.

To begin an **InPrivate browsing** session:

1 In Microsoft Edge, click the **...** (**Settings and more**) button on the menu bar

2 Select the **New InPrivate window** option

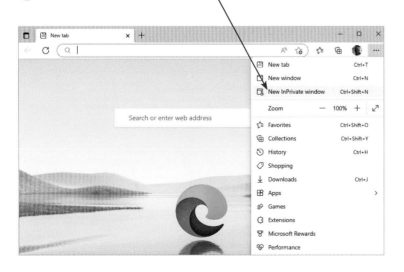

You can also press the **Ctrl** + **Shift** + **P** keys to open a new **InPrivate** window.

While **InPrivate browsing** keeps other people who use your computer from seeing which sites you've visited, it does not prevent someone on your network, such as a network administrator, from accessing this information.

Hiding your drives

The following procedure does more than just hide a file or folder – it actually hides the drive where the file/folder is located. For example, we can hide **Drive E** from the system shown here:

Hot tip

If you are going to be hiding and unhiding a drive on a regular basis, having to go into the Registry each time will be a pain. So, instead, you can create a shortcut:

Create a **NoDrives** DWORD, as described, and give it a value of 0. Then, right-click the **Explorer** folder on the left and click **Export**. In the **File name** box, type "Unhide.reg", then save it to the desktop.

Next, go back to the **NoDrives** DWORD, and in the **Value data** box enter the number of the drive to be hidden. Return to the **Explorer** folder and export it with the name **Hide.reg**.

Now, just click the **Hide** icon to conceal the drive and the **Unhide** icon to reveal it (not forgetting to restart the PC).

1 Start the Registry Editor and locate the following key:
HKEY_CURRENT_USER\SOFTWARE\Microsoft\Windows\CurrentVersion\Policies

2 Right-click the **Policies** folder and click **New > Key**, then name the new key **Explorer**

3 Click the **Explorer** folder, and on the right, right-click and select **New > DWORD (32-bit) Value**, then name it **NoDrives**

4 Double-click **NoDrives** to open the **Edit** dialog, then choose a base value of **Decimal**

5 Now, in the **Value data** box, enter the number of the drive to be hidden from the values in the table below (for example, for **Drive E** enter **16**)

Drive A – 1	Drive J – 512	Drive S – 262144
Drive B – 2	Drive K – 1024	Drive T – 524288
Drive C – 4	Drive L – 2048	Drive U – 1048576
Drive D – 8	Drive M – 4096	Drive V – 2097152
Drive E – 16	Drive N – 8192	Drive W – 4194304
Drive F – 32	Drive O – 16384	Drive X – 8388608
Drive G – 64	Drive P – 32768	Drive Y – 16777216
Drive H – 128	Drive Q – 65536	Drive Z – 33554432
Drive I – 256	Drive R – 131072	All – 67108863

The dashes in this table are not a minus sign; just enter the numeric value listed.

6 Click **OK**, then restart the PC, or sign out then back in, to implement the change

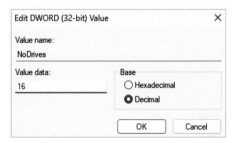

Decimal values are provided here but you could use their hexadecimal equivalent. For example, decimal 16 is hexadecimal 10.

7 Open **File Explorer > This PC** then choose **Devices and drives** to see that the drive is now hidden

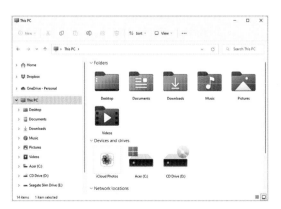

To unhide a drive, return to the **NoDrives** key in the Registry Editor then enter **0** in its **Value data** box.

Hiding your private files

Users who want to hide a file or folder quickly can do so by means of the Windows **Hidden Files and Folders** feature. While this is intended primarily to conceal important system files, which if modified or deleted can cause damage to the operating system, it can also be used to hide other files or folders.

1 Right-click the file to be hidden and click **Properties**

2 On the **General** tab, check the **Hidden** box in the **Attributes** section

3 Click the **Apply** button and the file icon will disappear

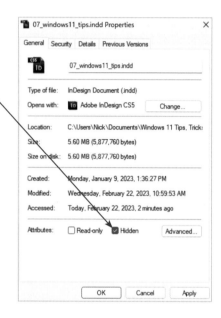

Beware

The method described on this page, while useful, is no means secure. Anyone who knows about this feature will be able to access anything you hide in this way.

4 To show the hidden file, go to **File Explorer > Folder Options**. Click the **View** tab, and check **Show hidden files, folders, and drives**, as shown on page 75

5 Click the **Apply** button and the file icon will reappear

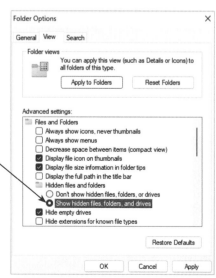

8 Security

PC owners these days face an unprecedented level of threats to their data. This chapter explains what they are and how to guard against them. There is also the issue of your family's safety and how to protect them from digital dangers.

Most laptops provide a connector to which a cable can be connected to secure them.

Locking devices for removable media drives are also available. These are mounted on the front panel of the drive and prevent access to it.

Securing your PC physically

One of the most glaring security loopholes of all is physical theft. The PC's data may be well secured, but what's to prevent someone from simply tucking the system case under their arm and walking away with it? They may not be able to access the data on the PC but you've still lost it.

While your home insurance (if you have it – many don't – and assuming it pays out) will cover the cost of replacing the PC, it won't replace your data.

So, if yours is irreplaceable, and you are not in the habit of creating up-to-date backups on separate media (writable discs, USB flash drives, etc.) or cannot afford to be without the PC for the length of time needed to replace it, then you need to physically secure it.

The following methods are available:

Alarms
These are the least effective method as they don't provide any physical restraint, but may be sufficient to deter the casual thief. A typical system will consist of a motion sensor that you fix to the system case. If someone tries to open the case or pick it up, an alarm will be triggered.

Cables
A cable system consists of plates, which are fixed to the case and peripherals by bolts or industrial-strength adhesive. The cable is fixed to one plate, looped through the others and then fixed to an anchor plate on the desk. To steal the PC, the thief will have to steal the desk along with it. They can, however, open the case and steal all the components inside.

Enclosures
These are lockable heavy-duty metal boxes into which the system case is placed, and are secured to the desk by bolts or adhesive. This is the best method, as not only is it impossible to steal the PC, but it is also impossible to open the case and steal the PC's components.

So, if you want to keep both the PC and the data it contains safe, take steps to physically secure it.

Restricting access to Windows

The next step is to prevent access to the operating system. Here are two ways to do this:

Setting a Boot password

Most BIOS setup apps provide an option to password-protect the bootup procedure. To do this, start the PC and enter the BIOS setup app – see page 58.

On the opening screen you should see a **Set User Password** option. Select this and enter a password – this password-protects the BIOS setup app. Then, look for a security option (usually found in the **Advanced BIOS Features** page). This enables you to set a Boot password. Do so, save the changes, and exit the BIOS. Now, bootup will stop at the Boot screen and ask you to enter the password.

Setting a Sign-in password

During the installation routine of Windows 11, the user is asked to specify a password. However, this is only mandatory if using a Microsoft account – if you set up Windows using a Local account, a password is not necessary.

If the latter option was taken when the PC was set up, you can set a password now, as described below:

  Go to **Settings** > **Accounts**, then click **Sign-in options**

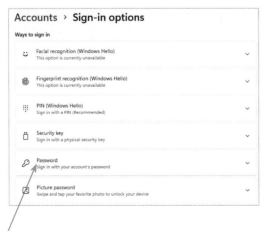

Password-protecting the BIOS setup app as well means a hacker has two passwords to crack before the PC can be booted up.

If you choose not to sign in with a Microsoft account, some features of Windows 11 will be unavailable to you.

You may choose to sign in to Windows 11 with a regular password, a PIN, or a picture password.

119

 Under **Password**, click the **Add** or **Change** button, then follow the prompts to create or change a password

Keeping your passwords safe

Most computer users these days will have several passwords – many will have a dozen or more. It can be difficult to remember these passwords, particularly those that are rarely used. Accordingly, many users keep a file on the PC that contains all their passwords.

However, while this ensures they don't forget them, a new problem arises – password theft. Unfortunately, Windows does not provide a utility that can be used to safely store and manage passwords.

So, what we suggest is that you acquire a password manager app. The easiest way is to download one from the internet – you will find literally hundreds – some free, some not. The one shown below, **Dashlane**, is a typical example.

These apps work by hiding passwords behind asterisks; a mouse click is required to reveal them. Thus, malicious software will not be able to see what they are. The password managers themselves are also password-protected to prevent physical access by a snooper. So, all you have to do is remember a single password.

The **Dashlane** password manager is available free online for download from dashlane.com

A password manager will need you to supply a "master password", which you must remember to keep safe.

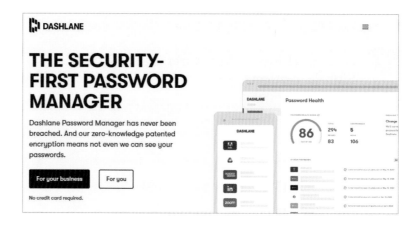

Good password managers have an autofill facility, similar to Microsoft Edge's **Autofill**. It should also be possible to install and run them from removable media. A good example is **RoboForm**, which can be used from a flash drive.

The **RoboForm** password manager is available free online for download from roboform.com

Encrypting your private data

We've seen how to secure your data by password-protecting both it and the PC. What we haven't considered yet is the possibility of someone cracking your password. The answer to this is to encrypt the data itself, thus adding a further layer of protection.

Windows 11 provides data encryption via its **Encrypting File System (EFS)** feature, and it's very easy to use. Simply right-click the folder containing files to be encrypted and click **Properties**. Then, click the **Advanced** button, and in the dialog box that opens, select **Encrypt contents to secure data**. When the encryption has finished, the names of the encrypted files will change to green, signifying that they are encrypted.

However, even though it is encrypted, the data is still vulnerable to someone who either physically steals the entire PC or the drive the data is stored on. This is due to the fact that EFS only works on drives formatted with the NTFS file system, so if the encrypted folder is copied to a non-NTFS drive, the encryption is removed and the data will thus be accessible.

To guard against this, you need to use another feature provided by Windows 11. This is called **BitLocker Drive Encryption** and it provides offline data protection by making it possible to encrypt an entire drive (including removable USB flash drives).

Go to **Control Panel** and click **BitLocker Drive Encryption**. Click **Turn on BitLocker** next to the drive to be encrypted and then follow the prompts – this will include setting a password to unlock the drive. Note that the encryption

> BitLocker Drive Encryption
> Help protect your files and folders from unauthorized access by protecting your drives with BitLocker.
>
> Operating system drive
>
> Acer (C:) BitLocker off
>
> 🔓 Turn on BitLocker

process can take a very long time. When it is finished, if you go to **This PC**, you will see that the encrypted drive now has a padlocked drive icon.

If you remove the drive and then reinstall it, a dialog box will pop up asking for the password.

To remove encryption or set a different method of unlocking the drive, re-open the utility and select **Turn off BitLocker**.

NTFS (New Technology File System) is the file system used by the Windows 11 operating system.

To access the **BitLocker Drive Encryption** option within the **Control Panel**, select **View by: Large icons/ Small icons** in the main **Control Panel** window and select it from the categories that appear.

Note that **BitLocker** cannot be used on a single file or folder. You have to encrypt the entire drive that contains the data to be protected.

Data backup

Another way in which your data can be compromised is by losing it. This can be through accidental deletion, a virus attack, hardware or operating system failure, or data corruption. As a safeguard against any of these potential threats, you need to create a backup on a separate medium. Traditionally, this has required a backup app, and Windows 8 provided an excellent imaging utility that was called Windows 7 File Recovery. However, in Windows 11 it has been removed because Microsoft is promoting the Cloud as a backup medium, via its **OneDrive** app. Therefore, anyone wishing to do image or large-scale backups in Windows 11 will do best to purchase a third-party utility. There are many good choices here, such as **Acronis True Image**. This offers image backups, continuous backups in real time, and many more features.

Windows itself offers just two methods of data backup: **File History** in the **Control Panel**, and the aforementioned **OneDrive** app. The latter is deeply integrated into Windows 11, which makes it very straightforward to use. For example, when you save a document with the **Save As** command, one option is **OneDrive**. Select this, and the file will be seamlessly uploaded to your **OneDrive** account, where it will be safe from whatever disaster may befall your PC. Furthermore, by default, your **Documents** folder is synced to your online **OneDrive** account, so files can be automatically backed up simply by placing them in the **Documents** folder. Thus, **OneDrive** provides an ideal method of backing up small files. The drawback is that the total amount of free storage is currently restricted to just 5GB, but you can buy an upgrade to 100GB, and an **Office 365** subscription includes up to 6TB of OneDrive storage, with a family subscription.

For those of you not up to speed with current computer terminology, "the Cloud" or "cloud computing" is a term for the delivery of hosted services over the internet. On this page it refers to the use of the free storage space provided by Microsoft, which users can use to safely store their data via the **OneDrive** app.

A big advantage of using **OneDrive** to back up your data is that once configured, the process is automatic – you'll never forget to do it, provided your Windows 11 device is online.

Right-click the **OneDrive** icon in the system tray, then choose **Settings**. Now, select the **Sync and backup** option in the left-hand sidebar and click **Manage backup** to configure the folders you want to sync.

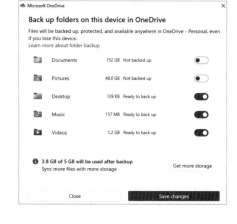

Microsoft OneDrive

Back up folders on this device in OneDrive

Files will be backed up, protected, and available anywhere in OneDrive - Personal, even if you lose this device.
Learn more about folder backup

Documents	152 GB	Not backed up	○
Pictures	48.0 GB	Not backed up	○
Desktop	139 KB	Ready to back up	●
Music	157 MB	Ready to back up	●
Videos	1.2 GB	Ready to back up	●

ⓘ 3.8 GB of 5 GB will be used after backup
Sync more files with more storage   Get more storage

Close   Save changes

Recovering your data

File History is a replacement for the "Previous Versions" utility found in some earlier versions of Windows, and allows users to quickly restore individual files that have been modified, damaged or even deleted.

It works by making automatic backups (every hour by default) of all files stored in the following folders: **Contacts**, **Desktop**, **Favorites**, and **Libraries**. All other folders are ignored. However, if you want to include a folder other than the default ones, all you have to do is place it in a library.

By default, **File History** is turned **Off**. Enable it as follows:

1 Connect an external drive to the PC. Typically, this will be a USB flash drive or an external hard drive

2 Go to **Control Panel** > **System and Security** > **File History**. Assuming you have correctly connected an external drive, you will see this:

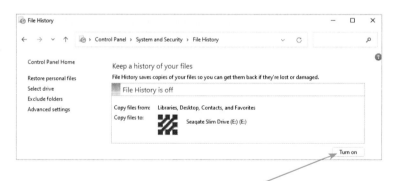

3 Now, click the **Turn on** button

All files in the above-mentioned folders will now be automatically backed up every hour. Existing backups are not overwritten by new ones – each backup is kept, so over a period of time a file history is created. This enables a file to be restored from a backup created at a specific hour and day.

To restore a file, click the **Restore personal files** link at the top left of the window. Then, browse to the required backup.

The only way to specify additional folders to be backed up is to add them to a library.

You can choose specific folders not to back up in **File History** by clicking the **Exclude folders** link.

By default, backups are made every hour. However, this can be changed by clicking **Advanced settings** and choosing a different interval, from **Every 10 minutes** to **Daily**.

Keeping Windows updated

While Windows 11 is currently a very secure operating system, rest assured that even as you read this, many people are working on ways to circumvent its security features, as they did with previous versions of Windows. To counter this, Microsoft releases a stream of automatic updates for Windows 11, which plug security loopholes as and when they are discovered.

If you have other Microsoft products installed it is convenient to also allow automatic updates for these, and you may additionally enable faster updates for all PCs on your local network.

1 Go to **Settings** > **Windows Update** > **Advanced options**, then drag **On** the **Receive updates for other Microsoft products** option

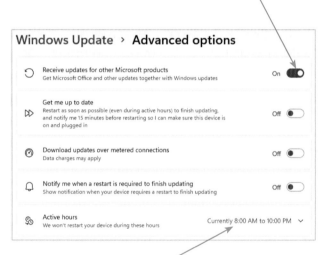

2 Click the **Active hours** option to specify times during which you do not want your devices to be automatically turned off and restarted

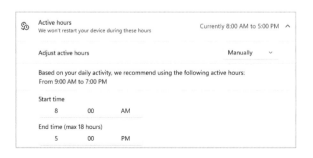

Privacy issues with Sync

A feature in Windows 11, and one that is sure to be popular with many users, is **Sync**. This enables settings and data to be synchronized across a number of Windows 11 devices. For example, you may have a Windows 11 PC on which you keep contact and email account details. By using the same Microsoft account on your Windows 11 Surface tablet, this data will be automatically copied to your tablet. Also, any subsequent changes to the data will be updated automatically; i.e. synchronized.

While this is undoubtedly convenient and will prove to be a real time saver for many users, there are sure to be occasions when it is not desirable from a security point of view. For instance, if several people have access to one of your devices, you may not want your website passwords synced. Another scenario is your **Personalization** settings, which, by default, will be synced and applied to all of your Windows 11 devices – this is something you may not want.

The solution is to configure the **Sync** feature to disregard settings you'd rather not share across your devices. Do it as follows:

Full synchronization allows your documents, photos, music, etc. to be accessible on all devices signed in with the same Microsoft account.

1 Go to **Settings** > **Accounts** > **Windows backup**

Synchronization lets your background, color, etc. settings be replicated across your devices.

2 Drag the **Remember my preferences** button **On** and check **On** the items that you would like to have available across different devices; e.g. **Passwords**

Windows Security

The source of many dangers to PC owners is the internet. The **Windows Security** center can be used to protect against some of these dangers, and also provide general security for your Windows computer. To use the **Windows Security** features:

1 Select **Settings** > **Privacy & security**

2 Click the **Windows Security** option, with the results listed under the **Protection areas** heading

Hot tip

Click the **Virus & threat protection** option in Step 2 to run a virus check over your computer.

Hot tip

A virus "definition" (a.k.a. virus signature) is a unique binary pattern that identifies a computer virus.

3 Click one of the **Protection areas** categories to view its options; e.g. **Device security**

4   Click the **Open
Windows Security**

Open Windows Security

button on the main
security page to open the **Windows Security** app

5   Click each item
to view its options
and use the left-
hand toolbar to
move between the
sections. Click
the **Home** button
to return to
this page

Using a firewall

A firewall can be used to help protect your network from viruses
and malicious software. To activate this:

1   Click the
**Firewall &
network
protection**
option on
the Windows
Security
homepage

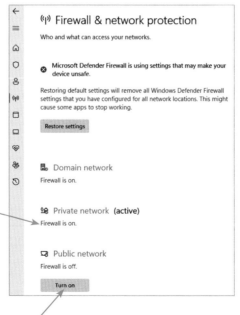

2   The related
networks are
listed, with their
firewall status;
e.g. **Firewall
is on**

3   If a firewall is **Off** for any item, click
the **Turn on** button to activate it

Turn on

Hot tip

The Microsoft Defender
Firewall can be used
to provide a level of
protection against
malicious software and
viruses.

Don't forget

Microsoft Defender
Firewall is on by default
in Windows 11, but you
can turn it off if you
have another firewall
installed and active.

...cont'd

Protecting against viruses

The Windows Security center can be used to give a certain amount of protection against viruses and malicious software. To activate this:

Malware (malicious software) is designed to deliberately harm your computer. To protect your system, you need up-to-date antivirus and anti-spyware software. The **Windows Security** option provides this, and you can also install a separate antivirus app.

1 On the Windows Security homepage click the **Virus & threat protection** option

Protection areas

Virus & threat protection
Actions recommended.

2 Click the **Quick scan** button to scan your system for viruses

○ Virus & threat protection

Protection for your device against threats.

🕔 Current threats

No current threats.
Last scan: 10/6/2021 9:54 AM (quick scan)
0 threat(s) found.
Scan lasted 15 minutes 11 seconds
42526 files scanned.

Quick scan

Scan options

Allowed threats

Protection history

3 Once the scan is completed, any threats will be noted and options for dealing with them listed; e.g. removing or quarantining items

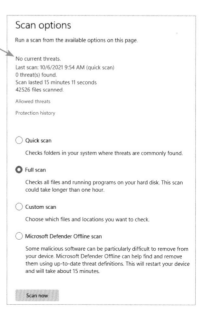

Scan options

Run a scan from the available options on this page.

No current threats.
Last scan: 10/6/2021 9:54 AM (quick scan)
0 threat(s) found.
Scan lasted 15 minutes 11 seconds
42526 files scanned.

Allowed threats

Protection history

○ Quick scan

Checks folders in your system where threats are commonly found.

● Full scan

Checks all files and running programs on your hard disk. This scan could take longer than one hour.

○ Custom scan

Choose which files and locations you want to check.

○ Microsoft Defender Offline scan

Some malicious software can be particularly difficult to remove from your device. Microsoft Defender Offline can help find and remove them using up-to-date threat definitions. This will restart your device and will take about 15 minutes.

Scan now

Click on the **Scan options** link in Step 2 to access options for more comprehensive scans over your computer.

Scan options

Device performance & health

The Windows Security center can also report on the general health of your Windows PC

1 Click the **Device performance & health** option in the left-hand sidebar

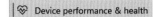

2 A **Health report** is displayed for your PC. This is generated automatically and any issues will be listed. If so, click on any item to view further details

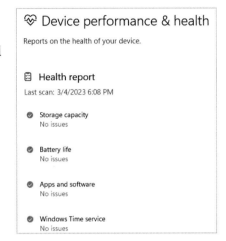

Family protection

Another function in the Windows Security center is for protection for family members using your PC with their own account. To use this:

1 Click the **Family options** option in the left-hand sidebar

2 The available **Family options** are listed. Click the **View family settings** option to open a web page in the Edge browser, where family safety settings can be applied

Don't forget

See pages 130-132 for more details about family safety options.

129

Family safety

The internet is a minefield that can expose naïve and trusting kids to many different types of threats. All responsible parents will want to minimize, if not eliminate completely, the risks to which their children are exposed. There are many commercially-available apps that help them to do this, such as **Net Nanny**. The best of these applications enable parents to control and monitor every aspect of what a typical child might want to do on a computer and the internet. Windows 11 provides its own family safety **Family** app (see pages 131-132) and there is also an option for adding accounts to your PC for other family members. To do this:

1 Go to **Settings** > **Accounts** > **Family**

2 Click the **Add someone** button, under the **Your family** heading

> Your family
>
> Add someone to your family group and allow them to sign in on this device   Add someone

3 Enter the child's email address, or click on the **No Microsoft account? Create one for a child** link to create a new account.
Follow the step-by-step wizard to create and complete the new account

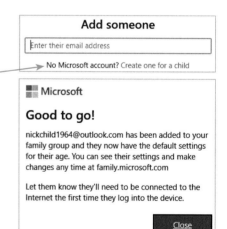

Add someone

Enter their email address

No Microsoft account? Create one for a child

Microsoft

Good to go!

nickchild1964@outlook.com has been added to your family group and they now have the default settings for their age. You can see their settings and make changes any time at family.microsoft.com

Let them know they'll need to be connected to the Internet the first time they log into the device.

Close

4 Click the **Close** button to complete the process

5 Return to **Settings** > **Accounts** > **Family** to see the new child account has been added to the **Your family** section

Beware

Before the child account is added to your family settings, the child may need to respond to an email invitation or sign in to a Windows 11 device for verification.

Family app

This provides a web-based control panel from which you can perform a number of tasks in terms of protecting children when they are using your computer and online. These include:

- Blocking/allowing specific websites.

- Using web filtering to block unsuitable content. Different filters can be created for each child.

- Blocking file downloads.

- Controlling and monitoring who your kids are communicating with via instant messaging software and email.

- Getting monitoring reports on what your kids have been doing, both on the internet and the PC.

- Accessing and adjusting each child's safety settings.

The **Family** app not only enables parents to control everything their kids do on the internet, but also provides a degree of protection to the PC by blocking potentially dangerous downloads, and access to apps and settings on the PC.

To get started with the **Family** app:

1 Go to **Settings > Accounts > Family** and click the **Open Family app** button. This takes you to the Microsoft Store, from where you can download the **Family** app

Microsoft Family
Manage family safety settings, see family activity, and more

Hi Nick! Explore Microsoft Family

Stay connected with loved ones and build healthy digital habits with Microsoft Family. Stay safer online, share photos, keep your devices secure, and more.

Open Family app   Learn more

Don't forget

There is also a Family Safety website, at **https://account. microsoft.com/family** that provides the same options as the **Family** app.

...cont'd

2 Click the **Get** button to download the **Microsoft Family Safety** app

Microsoft Family Safety

Microsoft Corporation

Get

3 Open the app and sign in with your Microsoft account details. All family members who have been added to your Microsoft account will be listed within the app. Click on a person's name to view the family safety options

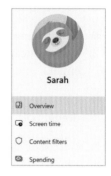

Sarah

⊞ Overview

ⓒ Screen time

◯ Content filters

▦ Spending

4 Click the **Content filters** option in Step 3 and drag the **Filter inappropriate websites and searches** button **On** to restrict mature web content

Filter settings

Filter inappropriate websites and searches

◉ On

Protect Sarah from mature content on the web and enable SafeSearch with Bing. When turned on, this setting will block other browsers and only allow Microsoft Edge.

You can unblock browsers in app and game filters.

5 Click the **Screen time** option in Step 3 to set time limits for when a child can use the device

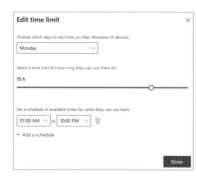

Edit time limit ✕

Choose which days to set limits on their Windows 10 devices

Monday ∨

Select a time limit for how long they can use them for:

15 h

Set a schedule of available times for when they can use them

07:00 AM ∨ to 10:00 PM ∨ 🗑

+ Add a schedule

Done

9 Some inner workings

This chapter focuses on installation and setting-up procedures, including the best ways to upgrade to Windows 11 and how to reset your PC.

Don't forget

Before carrying out a Windows reinstallation, make sure you back up your data. Although rare, an installation can result in data loss.

Hot tip

To run **Disk Defragmenter**, open **Computer/This PC** in File Explorer, then right-click on the drive icon and choose **Properties** > **Tools** > **Optimize and defragment drive** > **Optimize** – see page 43 for details.

Hot tip

To run **chkdsk**, open **Computer/This PC** in File Explorer, then right-click on the drive icon and choose **Properties** > **Tools** > **Error checking** > **Check** – see page 42 for details.

Upgrading to Windows 11

When installing a new operating system, the option taken by most users is to simply install it over the top of the old one – a procedure known as upgrading.

The drawback with this method is that problems in the existing setup will be carried over to the new one. Typical examples of this are viruses and malware. There may also be third-party apps on the old setup that are corrupted and thus cause problems; these may also be carried over to the new setup. Furthermore, these issues can cause the installation of the new operating system to fail.

For these reasons, the best way of updating your operating system is to completely remove the old one first. Then, you install the new version. This method is known as a "clean install". However, there is a drawback – the procedure wipes the hard drive clean of all data, so you first have to make a backup of any data you don't want to lose and then reinstall all of your applications.

Because of this, you may prefer to go down the upgrade route instead, in which case we suggest you first carry out the following steps. This will greatly improve the chances of doing it successfully:

1 Optimize your hard drive by running a disk defragmentation utility, such as Windows' **Disk Defragmenter**

2 Run a disk checking utility, such as Windows' **chkdsk** – hard drive errors are a common cause of installation problems

3 Check your system for viruses; these can stop an installation in its tracks. Having made sure your system is free of viruses, uninstall the antivirus app. Alternatively, you may be able to disable it in the BIOS. Antivirus software is well known for causing installation problems

4 Remove all apps from your **Startup** folder. Disconnect as much of your system's hardware as you can. Problems often occur during the hardware detection and configuration stages of an installation

Setting up user accounts

Windows allows the setting up of any number of user accounts, each of which can be individually configured in many ways (desktop icons, wallpapers, screen savers, and so on).

This feature is particularly useful in a home environment where several family members all use one PC. By giving each their own account, which they can customize to suit their specific requirements and tastes, a single PC can be used without conflict.

It can also be useful in a single-user environment by enabling a user to create accounts for specific purposes. For example, one account can be set up for photo editing, with shortcuts to all the relevant apps placed on the desktop. Another account can be set up as a home office, etc.

 Go to **Settings** > **Accounts** > **Other users**, then under **Add other user** click **Add account**

Accounts > **Other Users**

Other users

Add other user   Add account

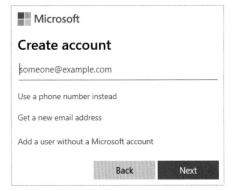

 You will now have options of signing in with an existing Microsoft account or creating a new one. You can also create a Local account by opting to sign in without a Microsoft account, plus create a child account

The disadvantages of a Local account are that the user won't be able to download apps from the Microsoft Store, and they won't be able to synchronize their settings and data across different devices and computers.

When two or more accounts are created, one of them must be an **Administrator** account. The person running this account will be able to set restrictions on what other account holders can and cannot do.

A useful application of user accounts is to password-protect the main account, and then create standard accounts for the kids. They can use the PC but won't be able to compromise its security or performance, due to the limitations placed on standard accounts.

Installing Windows 11 quickly

Here, we show you how to install Windows 11 from a USB flash drive. The advantages of installing Windows in this way are threefold:

- Speed – Windows will install much quicker.

- You will have a much more robust copy of the installation disk (which you can now put in a drawer and forget about).

- You can install Windows on PCs with no DVD drive.

Microsoft provides the **Windows 11 Installation Assistant**, which enables you to easily create bootable USB installation media.

1 Open your web browser and navigate to **microsoft.com/en-us/software-download/windows11**

2 Next, click the button labeled **Download Now**

Create Windows 11 Installation Media

If you want to perform a reinstall or clean install of Windows 11 on a new or used PC, use this option to download the media creation tool to make a bootable USB or DVD.

⊕ Before you begin

Download Now

---

3 When the download completes, select **Run** then click **Accept** to agree the license terms

4 On the **What do you want to do?** page, select **Create installation media for another PC**, then click **Next**

5 Now, choose the language, architecture, and edition you require (for example **English (US)**, **Windows 11**, **x64**), then click **Next** to continue

Don't forget

Before installing Windows 11 you should ensure the PC meets the system requirements for Windows 11 – see microsoft.com/en-us/windows/windows-11-specifications

Beware

Installation requires a product key. If you don't already have one you can select **I need to buy a product key** during the installation procedure.

6 On the **Choose which media to use** page, select the **USB flash drive** option

The USB drive must have a capacity of no less than 8GB and should be blank – any existing data already on the drive will be lost in this process.

7 Insert a USB drive, with a minimum capacity of 8GB, then click **Next**

8 Confirm the correct drive in the **Removable drives** list, then click **Next** to download Windows 11

9 When the download has completed, attach the USB drive to the PC where you want to install Windows 11

10 Restart the PC, then press any key to boot from the USB installation media

11 On the **Install Windows** page, select your language, time, and keyboard preferences, then click **Next**

12 Choose **Install Windows** and complete the step-by-step wizard process

Don't forget

To access the **Storage Spaces** option within the Control Panel, select **View by: Large icons/Small icons** in the main Control Panel window and select it from the categories that appear.

Hot tip

The advantage of an expandable space is simplified storage management.

Beware

One caveat with **Storage Spaces** is that they are not bootable; i.e. you cannot install an operating system on one.

Don't forget

You can mix and match drives of any type and size when creating **Storage Spaces**.

Creating a virtual drive

Of critical importance in the increasingly digital world is how to keep digital data safe. Related factors include how and where to store the data and the cost of doing so.

Within Windows there is a technology known as RAID (Redundant Array of Independent Disks), which can be used to provide data protection. RAID is available in either software or hardware versions and, of the two, hardware is by far the most reliable, as it is completely independent of the operating system. The problem with hardware RAID is that it requires a separate RAID controller card, and good ones are not cheap.

A feature in Windows 11 provides a much more cost-effective method of data protection, although, being a software solution, it is still not as robust as hardware RAID. The feature is known as **Storage Spaces** and can be accessed in the **Control Panel**.

Storage Spaces provides three very useful benefits – an easily-expandable space in which to store data, RAID data protection, and low cost.

Expandable space

A **Storage Space** is essentially a virtual drive comprised of a number of physical drives. The drives can be of any type, e.g. SATA, USB, SAS, etc., and of any size. The capacities of the drives are combined to produce a **Storage Space**. The capacity of the **Storage Space** can be increased at any time by simply adding another drive – this is its main advantage; a single drive of unlimited capacity can be created quickly and easily.

The capacity of a **Storage Space** is set by the user, and it is not restricted to the total capacity of the physical drives. For example, a 100GB **Storage Space** can be created from 10GB of physical drive space. This is achieved with a technique known as "thin provisioning", which gives the appearance of more space than actually exists. As more data is added to the **Storage Space** or virtual disk, the size of the real file grows as necessary.

When the capacity of a **Storage Space** has been used up, it can be reset to a larger size.

Data protection

When a Storage Space is created, the user has the option to add data protection of the same type used in RAID.

Three types of fault tolerance are offered: **Simple** (striping), **Mirror** and **Parity** (see Hot tips). For example, with two-way mirroring, two copies of a space's data are stored on separate drives. Thus, if one drive fails, the data is recoverable from the other.

Cost

Storage Spaces offers nothing that cannot be found elsewhere – there are quite a few other companies offering similar products. However, without exception, these cost hundreds of dollars, require specific hardware, and provide expansion options that are limited in scope.

Storage Spaces, on the other hand, costs nothing, requires no hardware other than the drives, provides a virtual drive of unlimited size, and is very simple and quick to set up. The procedure is outlined here:

1 Go to **Control Panel** > **Storage Spaces**, then choose **Create a new pool and storage space** – to see the drives on your system that are compatible with **Storage Spaces**

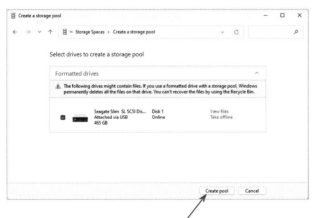

2 Select the drives you want to use for the **Storage Space** and click **Create pool**

3 In the new window, you will see options for the drive letter to use, the type of resiliency (simple, two-way mirror, etc.), and the size of the pool. When you have made your choices, click **Create Storage Space**

Simple spaces require at least one drive but don't make copy files, so are best for temporary data.

Mirror spaces (two-way) require two drives and make two copies of your files. They are best for general-purpose data.

Parity spaces require three drives and make multiple copies of your files. These are best for archive data and streaming media.

Simple spaces don't protect your data from drive failure, but **Mirror** spaces and **Parity** spaces can tolerate one drive failure – so they do protect your data.

Keeping your files and settings

Transfer everything to easily keep your user accounts, settings, documents, music, email, pictures, and video.

Don't forget

Install **PCmover Express** on both your old and new computers. Run the utility and select the transfer connection type. Follow the wizard steps, and your new computer will have the same personality and functionality as your old one.

140

Hot tip

Choose to transfer via Wi-Fi or Ethernet cable. Another good way is to use a Laplink USB cable (this has a USB plug on either end).

One of these days you're going to decide that you need a new computer. Having bought it, you will then need to redo all of the customization and configuration settings, such as internet/email settings, display settings, Taskbar configuration, and so on. You will also have to transfer all of your files, such as music and video, to the new PC. It will be a time-consuming process.

The **OneDrive** app in Windows 11 will help enormously. By default, all of your personalization and app settings, plus other stuff such as internet favorites and history, passwords, and many other Windows settings are automatically saved to your **OneDrive** storage account. All you have to do is configure the new PC with the same Microsoft account used on the old PC, and all the settings will be seamlessly transferred to it.

With regard to transferring your data, this is easy with the **PCmover Express** utility. This can be accessed at the **web.laplink.com** website. There are several versions of the utility: navigate to the required one, including one that can be downloaded from the Microsoft Store, and click the **Get** button.

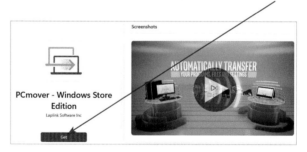

To transfer apps as well as data, download the **PCmover Professional** version.

Running older apps

When you install apps on your Windows 11 PC, you may come across one or two that refuse to run – this will be due to incompatibility issues. Before you give up on them, try installing them with the **Compatibility Troubleshooter** wizard. This will recreate the Windows environment for which they were designed and will, in most cases, get them running.

1 Go to **Control Panel > System and Security > Security and Maintenance**. At the bottom left, click **Windows Program Compatibility Troubleshooter**, then click **Next**

2 After a few moments you will see a dialog box showing you a list of all the apps on the PC. Select the one you're having trouble with, and then click **Next**

3 Select the app that won't run, then click **Next**

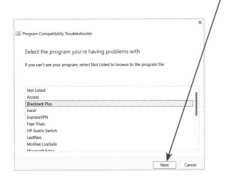

4 Now, click **Troubleshoot program** to check the selected app for any issues. In some cases you will be offered options for fixing any issues

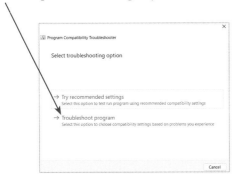

Once an app has been set up successfully, it will use the compatibility settings every time it is run.

If an app won't install at all, the method described here won't work. In this case, do it as described in the Hot tip below.

Another way of applying compatibility settings is to right-click the app's executable (setup) file. Click **Properties** and then open the **Compatibility** tab. From here, you can choose an operating system that the app is known to work with.

Calibrating your monitor

Have you ever noticed when printing an image that the print-out looks somewhat different from the image on the PC – for example: it's brighter or darker, the colors aren't the same, or it looks washed out?

It could be that the printer settings are not correct, but it's far more likely that your monitor is incorrectly calibrated. Windows 11 includes a monitor calibration utility – you can access it by going to **Settings** and entering **Display Color Calibration** into the Search box. Click the result. You will then be taken through a series of dialog boxes:

Before calibrating your monitor, allow the monitor to warm up for at least 30 minutes so that it's at its full operating temperature. This will ensure a consistent display.

142

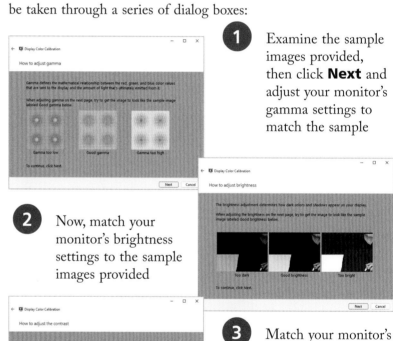

1 Examine the sample images provided, then click **Next** and adjust your monitor's gamma settings to match the sample

2 Now, match your monitor's brightness settings to the sample images provided

3 Match your monitor's contrast settings to the sample images provided

When calibrating your monitor, set your desktop background to a neutral gray. Bright colors and patterns surrounding an image make it difficult to accurately perceive color.

4 Finally, match your monitor's color-balance settings and save the new configuration

10 Shortcuts

This chapter contains some great tips for performing all of your favorite tasks faster and more efficiently.

Switching applications quickly

A useful feature in Windows 11 is the **Task View** option. This is located on the Taskbar and can be used to view all open apps and also add new desktops. To use **Task View**:

1 Click this button on the Taskbar

2 **Task View** displays minimized versions of the currently-open apps and windows

3 As more windows are opened, the format is arranged accordingly

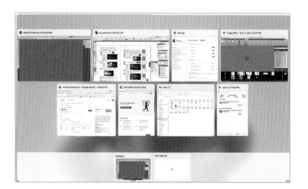

4 If an app has more than one window open (e.g. File Explorer), each window is displayed within **Task View**

5 Click a window in **Task View** to make it the active window

Hot tip

You can also access **Task View** by pressing **WinKey** + **Tab**, and you can move between desktops by holding down **Ctrl** + **WinKey** then pressing the **Left** or **Right** arrow keys.

Hot tip

The old **Flip** feature is still available too – hold down **Alt** then press **Tab** to switch between desktop thumbnails of your running apps.

Adding desktops

Another function within Task View is for creating additional desktops. This can be useful if you want to separate different categories of tasks on your computer. For instance, you may want to keep your open entertainment apps on a different desktop from your productivity ones. To create additional desktops:

1 Click the **Task View** button on the Taskbar

2 The current desktop is displayed

3 Click the **New desktop** button

4 The new desktop is displayed at the bottom of the **Task View** window

5 Click on the new desktop to access it. Each desktop has the same background and shortcuts

6 Open apps on the new desktop. These will be separate from the apps on any other desktop

One-click shutdown/restart

Users who like to do things quickly will appreciate the following methods of instantly shutting down, restarting or signing off.

Shutting down

Beware

Be sure to type these commands precisely, including spaces, or they will not work.

1 Create a desktop shortcut (right-click, **New > Shortcut**) and type **SHUTDOWN -s -t 01**

2 Click **Next**, name the shortcut **Shut Down**, then click **Finish**

Restarting

As above but this time type **SHUTDOWN -r -t 01** in the box. Name this shortcut **Restart**.

Signing off

As above, but this time type **SIGNOUT** in the box. Name it **Signout**.

When you have finished, you will see these icons on the desktop:

Hot tip

Drag the icons to the Taskbar to make them more readily accessible.

Using the steps detailed on page 107, you can change the icons to something more interesting or representative, as shown below:

Hotkey shortcuts

There will be occasions when you want to open an app, but don't wish to close the current window to get to it. For example, you may be doing a tax return online and need to open the calculator.

A hotkey shortcut is the answer.

1 Right-click the desktop and choose **New > Shortcut**, then type **calc.exe** in the location box

2 Click **Next** and name the shortcut **Calculator**, then click the **Finish** button

3 Now, right-click the shortcut icon and select **Properties** – to open its **Properties** dialog box

4 Click in the **Shortcut key** box (this will be reading **None**)

5 Now, do not type into the box, but simply press the key you want to use as the shortcut key – we pressed the **C** key in the example here

6 The **Shortcut key** box will now read **Ctrl + Alt + C**

7 Click **Apply** then click **OK**. From now on, you can open the application by pressing **Ctrl + Alt + C**

Hot tip

You can use the steps on this page to open your favorite websites with a combination keystroke. Create a shortcut with a web page URL in the location box. Right-click the shortcut, choose **Properties** and click the **Web Document** tab. Then, follow Steps 4-7 to assign a shortcut key to the web page.

147

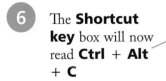

Hot tip

If your keyboard came with a software disk, you may find that it contains an app that enables you to create hotkey shortcuts with the **F** keys.

Windows key shortcuts

Most standard keyboards have one or even two Windows keys. These are situated near the space bar and have a logo of a flying window printed on them. The keys are commonly known as the **WinKey**.

Hot tip

On its own, press the **WinKey** at any time to open the Start menu.

Windows keys

With either of these keys you can quickly open a number of applications on your computer.

The table below shows which keys can be used in conjunction with the Windows key and what they do:

Hot tip

Keyboard shortcuts can also be found within applications. Alongside most menu commands, you will see shortcut key combinations.

148

Keys	Action
WinKey + Tab	Open/close Task View
WinKey + A	Open/close Quick Settings panel
WinKey + C	Open Chat app
WinKey + D	Minimize/restore all windows
WinKey + E	Open File Explorer displaying the Home folder
WinKey + I	Open Windows Settings
WinKey + L	Lock the computer
WinKey + N	Open Notification Center
WinKey + P	Open Project screen options
WinKey + R	Open the Run dialog box
WinKey + S	Open Search
WinKey + T	Cycle through Taskbar apps
WinKey + U	Open Accessibility settings
WinKey + X	Open the Power User menu

Keyboard shortcuts

In certain situations, using the keyboard can be a much easier way of controlling a computer. The following is a selection of useful keyboard shortcuts that will work in most situations, but not all:

General shortcuts	
Ctrl + A	Select all items in a document or window
Ctrl + C	Copy the selected item
Ctrl + N	Create a new document from within an app
Ctrl + O	Open a document from within an app
Ctrl + S	Save the current document within an app
Ctrl + V	Paste the selected item
Ctrl + W	Close the current document
Ctrl + X	Cut the selected item
Ctrl + Z	Undo the last action
Delete	Delete the selected item
Shift + Delete	Delete an item permanently
F2	Rename the selected item in File Explorer
Ctrl + Right arrow	Move to the beginning of the next word
Ctrl + Left arrow	Move to the beginning of the previous word
Ctrl + Down arrow	Move to the beginning of the next paragraph
Ctrl + Up arrow	Move to the beginning of the previous paragraph
Ctrl + Shift + arrow	Select text (depending on which arrow key is used)
F3	Search for a file or folder in File Explorer
Alt + Enter	Display properties for the selected item in File Explorer
Alt + space bar	Open the shortcut menu for the active window
Ctrl + F4	Close the active document
Alt + Tab	Switch between open items
Alt + Esc	Cycle through items in the order they were opened
F4	Display the address bar list in File Explorer
F5	Refresh an Edge browser window
F6	Cycle through screen elements in File Explorer
Right arrow	Open the menu to the right, or open a sub-menu
Left arrow	Open the menu to the left, or close a sub-menu
Alt + Up arrow	View the folder one level up in File Explorer
Esc	Cancel the current task
Ctrl + Shift + Esc	Open Task Manager
Shift (when inserting a CD)	Prevent the CD from automatically playing

The **Alt** + **Tab** shortcut doesn't need both keys pressed at once – hold down the **Alt** key then press the **Tab** key to switch between thumbnails.

...cont'd

Microsoft Edge shortcuts	
Tab	Move forward through items
Shift + Tab	Move backward through items
Alt + Home	Go to your homepage
Alt + Right arrow	Go to the next page opened in the tab
Alt + Left arrow	Go to the previous page opened in the tab
Up arrow	Move upward through the elements of a web page
Down arrow	Move downward through the elements of a web page
Ctrl + Home	Move to the beginning of a web page
Ctrl + End	Move to the end of a web page
Enter	Activate a selected link
F4	Display a list of recent searches
F5	Refresh the current web page
F12	Open/Close Developer Tools
Esc	Stop downloading a page
Ctrl + D	Add the active site to Favorites
Ctrl + E	Open search from the address bar
Ctrl + F	Find on this page
Ctrl + H	Open History
Ctrl + J	Open Downloads
Shift + Ctrl + K	Duplicate current tab
Ctrl + N	Open new window
Ctrl + Shift + N	Open new InPrivate window
Ctrl + Shift + O	Open Favorites
Ctrl + P	Open Print dialog
Ctrl + R	Restore current page
Ctrl + click	Open links in a new tab in the background
Ctrl + Shift + click	Open links in a new tab in the foreground
Ctrl + T	Open a new tab in the foreground
Ctrl + Tab	Switch between tabs
Ctrl + W	Close current tab
Alt + Enter	Open the **Settings and more** menu
Ctrl + 9	Switch to the last tab
Ctrl + F4	Close active tab
Alt + D	Select the text in the address bar
Ctrl + Enter	Add "www." and ".com"

Hot tip

The list on this page contains just some of the keyboard shortcuts available for Microsoft Edge and Internet Explorer. You can find many more by going to **support.microsoft. com/en-us/windows/ keyboard-shortcuts-in- windows-dcc61a57- 8ff0-cffe-9796- cb9706c75eec**

11 The internet

The internet is a wonderful resource for information, entertainment, software and business. This chapter details a wide range of tips that include extending the basic functionality of Microsoft Edge, useful features of this powerful browser, and how to improve the efficiency with which you use the internet.

No more broken downloads

Anyone who downloads data from the internet will, at one time or another, experience the irritation of an unexpected disruption to their download.

Unfortunately, Microsoft Edge doesn't have the ability to automatically resume interrupted downloads, so you then have to initiate the process again. This is not too bad if it is a small download, but if you are downloading a large file, you could waste a lot of time.

The solution is to use what's known as a download manager. Apps of this type monitor a download, and if it is interrupted for whatever reason will resume it from the point at which the download stopped – thus, you don't have to start again from the beginning.

Download managers also offer other useful features, such as automatic scheduling, automatic redial (for dial-up modem connections) and details regarding file size, download time, and so on.

One popular download manager app is **Download Accelerator Plus (DAP)**, available at **speedbit.com**

A good download manager can also increase download speeds. If the file is held on several servers (which is quite common), the app will switch between the servers, automatically selecting the one that offers the best – i.e. fastest – download conditions.

Cutting down on scrolling

Have you ever opened one of those web pages that seems to go on forever? To find something specific, you have to keep scrolling down the page and, if you miss it, then scroll back up.

Let's say you are researching an article on the Confederate States of America. Your search leads you to one of these long pages, the content of which is the American Civil War. All you want is information about the Confederate States, and nothing else. So, instead of endless scrolling down the page to find references to them, try the following:

1 On the keyboard, press **Ctrl + F**

Just below the address box, you will now see a **Find** toolbar.

2 Type **Confederate** into the Search box

You can also open the **Find** toolbar in Microsoft Edge by pressing the **F3** function key.

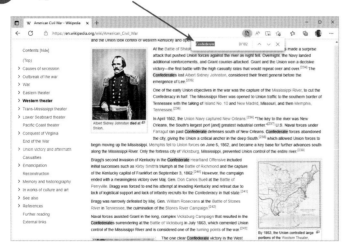

The **Find** feature will automatically scroll the page up and down as you click the arrow buttons to reveal the next instance found.

Microsoft Edge will automatically highlight all text instances of the word or phrase entered in yellow – so you can't miss them. Additionally, it displays a count of the total number of instances found alongside the Search box on the **Find** toolbar.

3 To go to the next instance found, press the **Down** arrow button that appears after the counter display

4 Press the **Down** arrow button to move to the next instance, or press the **Up** arrow button to return to the previous one

You can also navigate the search results using keyboard shortcuts. Hit **Enter** to move forward or **Shift** + **Enter** to move back, and hit **Esc** to exit the search.

File sharing

File sharing is a very popular internet activity. It makes use of specialized peer-to-peer networks and software, which allow users to connect directly to the computers of other users in the same network. The purpose of it all lies in the name – file sharing. Each user can designate specific files on their PC that they are willing to share.

To take part in this activity, you need a file-sharing app. These are available as a free download on the internet and there are dozens of them: enter **file sharing** into Google on the web.

Simply download and install the app, designate which files you want to share with other users, and you're all set to go. Good examples of this type of application are **BitLord** (**bitlord.com**) and **Emule** (**emule-project.net**).

Of all the file-sharing apps, **Emule** is considered to be one of the best. It also claims to be free of all adware and spyware – something that cannot be said for many of them.

Hot tip

To get the best out of file sharing, you really need a broadband connection, as many of the files available for download can be several gigabytes in size.

Beware

File-sharing networks are awash with viruses and malware. Not only that, but the file-sharing apps themselves may add malware to your system. Don't get involved in this activity if you want to keep your PC as clean as possible.

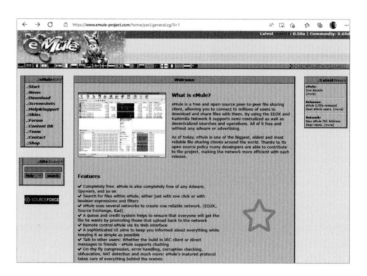

When using these apps, there are two things to be aware of:

- **Malware** – Some file-sharing apps may attempt to install malware onto your PC... be wary of this!

- **Copyright** – While the use of the app is legal, the downloading of copyrighted material is not... do this at your own risk!

Beware

Unauthorized copying or distribution of copyrighted material is illegal. Ensure you only share files legally.

Getting more search providers

A useful feature of Microsoft Edge is the ability to search directly from the address bar – there's no need to go to a search engine. Not surprisingly, though, results from a search are taken from Microsoft's search engine, **Bing**. Should you wish to use a different search engine, you can set this up as described below:

1 Open Microsoft Edge and click the **... (Settings and more)** button, then choose the **Settings** option

2 Click the **Privacy, search, and services** option in the left-hand sidebar

3 Scroll down to the **Services** section and click on **Address bar and search**

> **Address bar and search**
> Manage search suggestions and search engine used in the address bar

4 Click in the **Search engine used in the address bar** box, to select a different search engine used in the Edge address bar when searching for items on the web

> Search engine used in the address bar.   Bing (Recommended, default) ∨
> Manage search engines   >

5 Click on a search option, as required – e.g. Google – to specify this as the one used in the Edge address bar

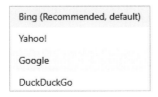

Hot tip

If outside the USA, entering the address **google.com** may redirect you to the local Google page of your country. If you do not want to do this, enter **google.com/ncr** (no country redirect) instead.

Quick internet searching

Type the word **tiger** into **Bing** or **Google** and you will get millions of pages to look through. These will range from the Tiger stores in Spain, to Tigerair in Singapore, to pages about tigers (the animals). Finding something specific may take a long time.

To help users narrow their searches, all of the major search engines offer an Advanced Search option. This will offer various options, such as language-specific searches, and searches restricted to pages updated within a specific time frame, etc.

However, before you try these, the following simple search aids may be all you need.

The + operator
Most search engines exclude common words such as "and" and "to", and certain single digits and letters. If you want to make sure a common word is included in the search, type **+** before it.

For example:

world war +1

(Make sure there is a space between the **+** sign and the previous word.)

The - operator

The - operator allows you to exclude words from a search. For example, if you are looking for windows (glass ones), type:

windows -microsoft

This will eliminate millions of pages devoted to the various Windows operating systems.

The or operator

The **or** operator allows you to search for pages that contain word A **or** word B **or** word C, etc. For example, to search for camping trips in either Yosemite or Yellowstone national parks, you would type the following:

"camping trips" yosemite or yellowstone

Phrase searches

By enclosing your keywords in quotation marks, you can do a phrase search. This will return pages with all the keywords in the order entered.

For example, **atlanta falcons** will return pages mainly concerning the Atlanta NFL team. Most pages regarding Atlanta (the city) or falcons (the birds) will be excluded.

Combinations of operators

To further narrow your searches, you can use combinations of search operators and phrase searches. Using our "atlanta falcons" example, you can remove several million search results by typing:

"atlanta falcons" -olympic games -birds of prey -city

Numeric range searches

Numeric range searches can be used to ensure that search results contain numbers within a specified range. You can conduct a numeric range search by specifying two numbers, separated by two periods with no spaces.

For example, you would search for computers in the $600 to $900 price bracket by typing **computers $600..900**.

Numeric range searches can be used for all types of units (monetary, weight, measurement, and so on).

You may, at some stage, come across the phrase "Boolean operators" with regard to search engines. These are derived from Boolean logic, which is a system for establishing relationships between terms. The three main Boolean operators are:

- **Or**
- **And** (equivalent to **+**)
- **Not** (equivalent to **-**)

157

The most useful operators are **-** (**Not**) and **quotation marks** (phrase searching). These two operators can whittle search results that would otherwise be several million down to a few hundred pages.

Easy text selection

When selecting text in a web page it can be difficult to select precisely what you want without also selecting adjacent text, and objects such as images and tables, as shown below:

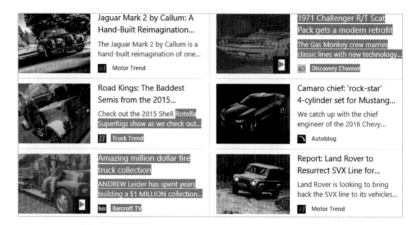

With Microsoft Edge, the **Caret Browsing** feature helps solve this problem. This lets you use the keyboard instead of the mouse to make selections, and it offers much more precise control.

1 Place the cursor at the beginning of the text block you want to select

2 Press **F7** to open the **Turn on caret browsing?** dialog box

3 Check **Don't ask me again when I press F7** if you want to use **Caret Browsing** often

> **Turn on caret browsing?**
> This lets you select text with your keyboard. Press F7 to turn this off.
> ☑ Don't ask me again when I press F7
> Turn on   Cancel

4 Next, click the **Turn on** button to activate **Caret Browsing**

5 Hold down the **Shift** key and highlight the text with the arrow keys

Getting to grips with tabs

Browser tabs are another useful feature in Microsoft Edge, whereby numerous web pages can be used within a single Edge window. When new tabs are opened, from this button at the top of the browser, the format is the same for all new tabs. This can be specified as follows:

1 Open Microsoft Edge and click the **...** (**Settings and more**) button, then choose the **Settings** option

2 Click the **Start, home, and new tabs** option in the left-hand sidebar

3 Scroll down to the **New tab page** section and click on the **Customize** button

4 Select options for inclusion in a new tab, as required. These include:

- **Quick links**
- **Background**
- **Recent Bing searches**
- **Show greeting**
- **New tab tips**
- **Content**
- **Feed view**

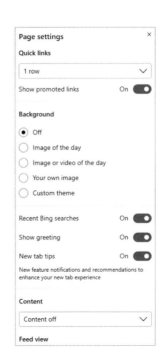

Hot tip

To close a specific tab when you have several open, you have to click the tab in order to reveal the **X** button. A quicker way is to click anywhere in the tab with the mouse's scroll wheel.

Hot tip

The settings selected in Step 4 will apply to the format for all new tabs.

...cont'd

Managing tabs

Once tabs have been opened in the Edge browser there are a number of options for viewing and managing them.

1 Right-click the new tab to view options for managing tabs, including creating a new tab, duplicating the currently-active tab, pinning tabs and changing the orientation of open tabs

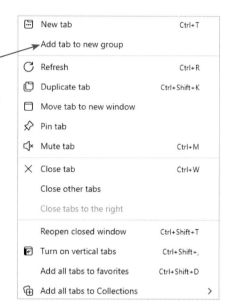

2 Click this button at the left-hand side of the tab bar to access more options

3 Click the **Turn on vertical tabs** option to change the orientation of the tab bar

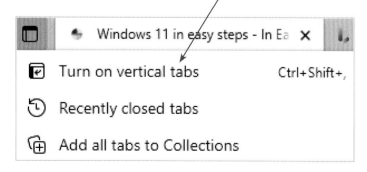

Click the **Add all tabs to Collections** option in Step 3 to add all of the open tabs to a Collection, which is a group of links to web pages.

4 The tab bar is displayed down the left-hand side of the Edge browser window

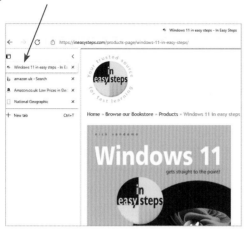

5 Click this button in Step 4 to minimize the vertical tab bar

6 Click this button to expand the minimized tab bar

The vertical tabs option can be used even if there is only one open tab.

7 Move the cursor over the minimized tab bar and click this button to expand it and keep the maximized option in place

Sharing pages

When you want to share a web page of interest, Microsoft Edge provides the ability to share a link to that page's URL address or a screenshot of the part of that page visible in your browser.

1 Open a web page and then click the **... (Settings and more)** button, then choose the **Share** option

2 In the **Share** panel, select how you would like to share the web page

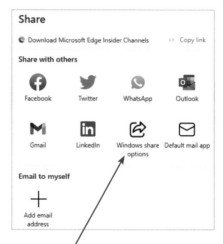

3 Click the **Windows share options** button in the previous step, to select options for sharing a link to the web page, including people nearby with compatible devices

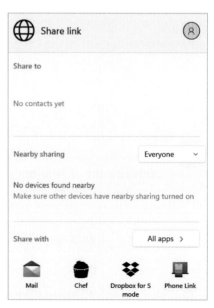

Becoming an Edge Insider

Updates to the Edge browser are being worked on continually, and you can be one of the first to view these, without having to wait for the next major upgrade to the browser. This is through the **Microsoft Edge Insider** option, which provides enlisted members with early release and beta versions of the browser. To make the most of this:

1 Click the **...** (**Settings and more**) button, then choose the **Settings** option

2 Click the **About Microsoft Edge** button in the left-hand sidebar

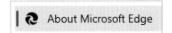

3 Click the **Learn more** button to find out more details about the **Insider** program

For each of the channels in Step 4 there is a description of what is included so that you can download the most appropriate version for your needs.

4 Click the **Download** button next to one of the options (**Beta Channel**, **Dev Channel** and **Canary Channel**) to obtain the latest versions of the Edge browser for each of these categories

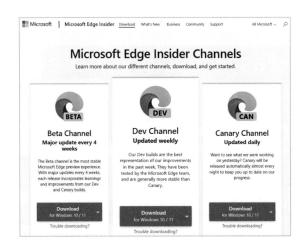

Web select

There is an amazing amount of useful information on the web, so it is not surprising that, from time to time, people want to copy some of the content from web pages and then use it in another app. One of the most common reasons for doing this is to copy text from a web page. This can be a hit-and-miss process, but the Edge browser makes it easier with the **Web select** function.

1 Click the **...** (**Settings and more**) button, then choose the **Web select** option

2 Drag around the text to be selected. This will be shown in individual text boxes. Click the **Copy** button

3 Open the required app, such as a word-processing app, and paste the text. It can now be edited in the normal way for text in a word-processing app

Web capture

The **Web capture** feature in the Edge browser is similar to the **Web select** one, in that it can be used to select and copy a specific area of a web page. However, **Web capture** saves this as one single image, and individual elements of the image cannot be edited. However, it is possible to draw on a **Web capture** image. To use **Web capture**:

1 Click the **...** (**Settings and more**) button, then choose the **Web capture** option

2 Select whether to capture the full web page or a selected **Capture area**

3 For **Capture area** drag around the area to be captured and click the **Copy** button

Once a markup drawing has been made on a **Web capture** image, click on these buttons in the top right-hand corner to, from left to right: share the image; copy the image; save the image on your PC.

4 To draw on the **Web capture** selection, click the **Markup capture** option

5 Click the **Draw** button to select options for drawing on the image

More Edge settings

There are numerous options for customizing the look and feel of the Edge browser, and also some of its functionality, using its settings. As a quick reminder, this is how to access them:

1 Click on the **...** (**Settings and more**) button and click **Settings** on the subsequent menu

2 Click on one of the main categories in the left-hand sidebar to view the options in the main window

Hot tip

You can also control the **Zoom** function with the keyboard:

- **Ctrl** plus **+** (plus sign) = zoom in by 25%

- **Ctrl** plus **-** (minus sign) = zoom out by 25%

- **Ctrl** plus **0** = zoom to default 100%

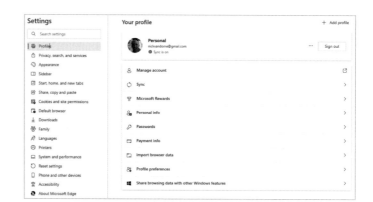

Changing the theme

Microsoft Edge offers an alternative to its default **Light** theme. Click **...** (**Settings and more**) > **Settings** > **Appearance**, then choose an option from the **Theme** section.

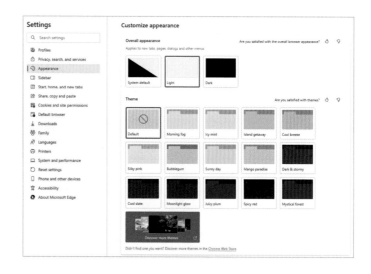

Seeing your Favorites

Websites saved into the **Favorites Bar** folder can be shown on the Microsoft Edge toolbar. Click **...** (**Settings and more**) > **Settings** > **Appearance**, then select the **Show favorites bar** option, from **Never, Always, Only on new tabs**.

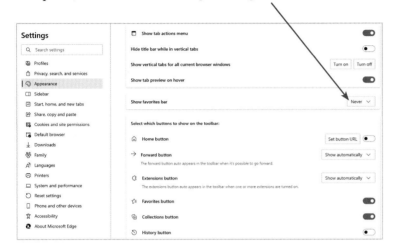

Pin the current web page to your **Start** menu as a tile that you can click to open, at any time, in a new tabbed window. Click **...** (**Settings and more**) > **More tools** > **Pin to Start** (or **Pin to taskbar**).

167

Providing a Home button

You can add a **Home** button on the Edge browser toolbar. Click **...** (**Settings and more**) > **Settings** > **Start, home, and new tabs**, then slide the **Show home button on the toolbar** toggle button from **Off** to **On**.

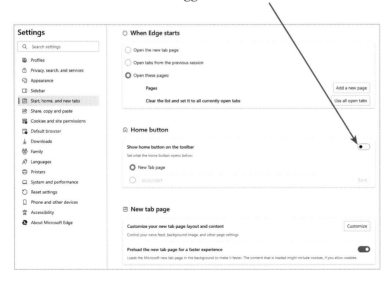

...cont'd

Customizing the sidebar

To display, and customize, the Edge browser sidebar, which appears at the right-hand side of the browser by default, click **...** (**Settings and more**) > **Settings** > **Sidebar**, then drag the **Show sidebar** button **On** or **Off**. Other selections can be made for notifications on the sidebar and also for the specific apps on it.

The Edge browser sidebar is different from the **Settings** sidebar, which is located at the left-hand side of the **Settings** window.

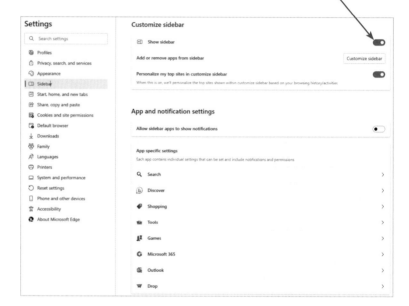

Applying Family Safety settings

You can access Family Safety settings as follows: click **...** (**Settings and more**) > **Settings** > **Family**, then click the **Manage your Microsoft Family Safety group** option.

For more details about using the **Family** app, see pages 130-132 in Chapter 8.

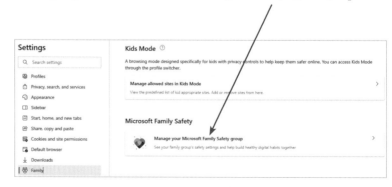

Edge extensions

Extensions are small apps that can give increased functionality to the Edge browser, such as blocking unwanted ads. There is a range of extensions that can be downloaded and used from a store similar to the Microsoft Store for regular apps. To add extensions to the Edge browser:

1 Click... (**Settings and more**) > **Extensions**

2 Click the **Open Microsoft Edge Add-ons website** option

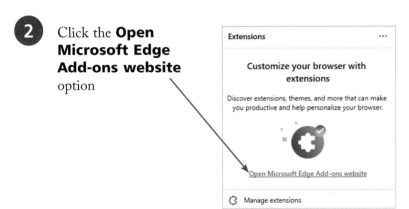

3 This takes you to the **Edge Add-ons** store

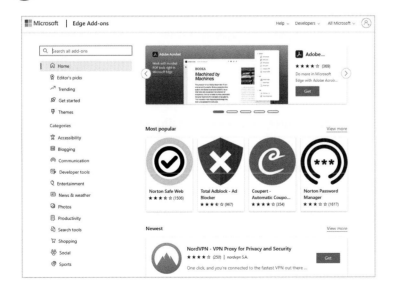

Don't forget

Use the left-hand sidebar to access the different categories within the **Edge Add-ons** store.

...cont'd

4 Click on an item to view more details about it

5 Additional information about the extension is displayed. Click the **Get** button if you want to use it

6 More information about the extension is displayed. Click on the **Add extension** button to add it to your Edge browser, where it will appear as an icon on the top toolbar of the browser

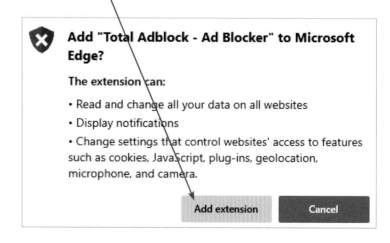

12 Email

In this chapter, we look at perhaps one of the most popular PC applications of all – email. Using the Outlook app, you will learn how to safeguard your messages and account settings, and how to mitigate against spam emails and viruses.

Setting up an email account

Windows 11 provides users with an email app called **Mail**. This provides few configuration options for the more advanced email user. If this is you, you may wish to install a third-party app. Mozilla, author of the Firefox web browser, provides the free **Thunderbird** email client, while another free email app with a very good reputation is **Eudora**. These can both be downloaded from the manufacturers' websites. If you do an internet search, you will also find a multitude of other email apps. This might be a good time to try out a few and see how you get on with them. Alternatively, you can opt to stay with Microsoft, with the **Outlook** mail app, which is a powerful email option and is included with an Office 365 subscription.

The Outlook mail app

To set up a first email account in Outlook:

1. Open the **Outlook** app and select **File > Info** from the top toolbar

Outlook

2. Click the **Add Account** button

3. To link an existing email account, enter the email address to use for the account, click on the **Connect** button, and follow the step-by-step wizard

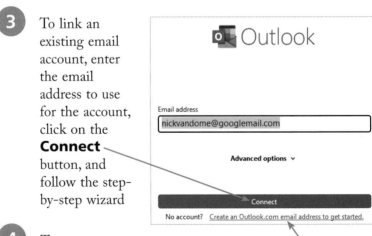

4. To create a new Outlook account with an Outlook email address, click **Create an Outlook.com email address to get started**

5 To set up an account manually, click the **Advanced options** button, check **On** the **Let me set up my account manually** checkbox, and click **Connect**

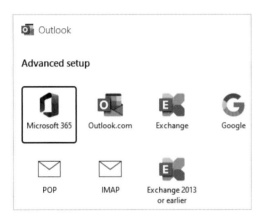

6 Select the type of email account that you want to set up

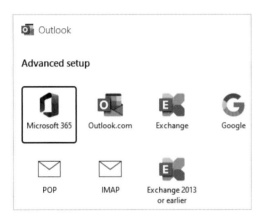

7 Enter the account details for the selected account. In some cases you will need to obtain these from your email account provider

If you are likely to use **Outlook** frequently, pin it to the **Start** menu and the Taskbar.

Using the Outlook Ribbon

The **Ribbon** has been a familiar feature in Windows File Explorer, although in Windows 11 this has been replaced with the File Explorer menu bar. However, the Ribbon format lives on in Outlook and it provides a range of options for managing the operation of Outlook. To use the Outlook Ribbon functionality:

1 For each of the Ribbon options, click this button at the right-hand side of the Ribbon and select options for how it is displayed and its layout

The **Simplified Ribbon** option in Step 1 reduces the size of the icons used with each item.

2 Click the **Home** button on the Outlook menu bar to access these options. They include creating new messages, deleting messages, replying to messages, moving messages, creating rules for when messages arrive, adding various tags to messages, and finding items within email messages

3 Click the **Send / Receive** button on the Outlook menu bar to access these options. They include specifying how messages are sent and received and also options for items that are downloaded as part of a message

4 Click the **Folder** button on the Outlook menu bar to access these options. They include creating new folders for storing emails, copying and renaming folders, marking items as read, reordering folders, adding items to your email favorites list, and selecting folder properties

5 Click the **View** button on the Outlook menu bar to access these options. They include changing the current inbox view and accessing settings for how mailboxes are displayed, showing email conversations, arranging emails according to date, sender, recipient, and size, and amending the layout view of the Outlook window

6 Click the **Help** button on the Outlook menu bar to access these options. They include online help options, online support, troubleshooting options, a feedback option for general comments about the Outlook app, training options, a **What's New** feature, general support tools, and a diagnostics option for identifying any problems or issues with the Outlook app

Don't forget

Email conversations consist of messages that are linked together through ongoing replies to an original message. A conversation can be viewed as one condensed item, with all subsequent messages available from the initial item.

Useful Outlook settings

Since Outlook is a powerful email app, it is understandable that it has a range of settings to match. These can be accessed as follows:

1 Open Outlook and on the Outlook menu bar select **File** > **Info**

2 Click the **Account Settings** button to view the relevant settings

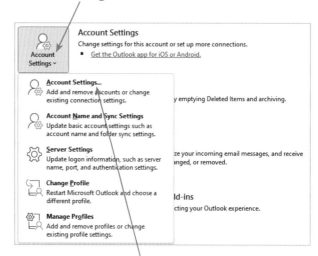

Hot tip

If you are having problems with your Outlook account, click the **Repair...** tab in Step 3 to run a step-by-step wizard aimed at fixing any problems with the account.

3 Click the **Account Settings...** option to view details of the available email accounts

4 Click the **Tools** button on the **Info** page (accessed in Step 1 on the previous page) and click on the **Mailbox Cleanup...** option to access options for managing your Outlook mailbox

5 Use the **Mailbox Cleanup...** option to access settings for managing the size of your mailbox and autoarchiving older items within Outlook

Click the **View Mailbox Size...** button in Step 5 to view how much space is being used by saved emails in different locations within Outlook.

177

6 Click the **Empty** button to remove deleted items permanently and click the **Yes** button to confirm the action

Backing up your emails

The provision of email facilities is a very important function of the modern-day computer, and just as people often like to keep personal letters, they also like to keep their emails. It is also an important means of business communication, and these messages usually need to be kept as records.

Outlook provides an easy way to back up your messages.

1 On the Outlook menu bar choose **File** > **Open & Export** – to see the **Open** screen

It's always a good idea to store backups on a separate medium. Email account settings are very small files, so a USB flash drive is ideal for backup.

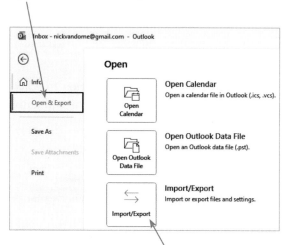

2 Next, click the **Import/Export** button – to launch the **Import and Export Wizard** dialog

3 Select the **Export to a file** option, then click **Next**

If you just want to back up a particular message, double-click it and select **Save As** from the **File** menu. You can then save it where you like.

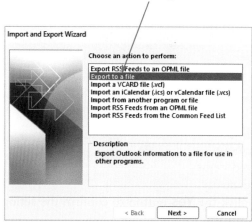

…cont'd

4 Now, select the compact **Outlook Data File (.pst)** file type (or **Comma Separated Values** for a text version), then click **Next**

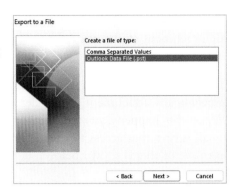

Comma Separated Values (CSV) files can usefully allow you to import messages into an Excel worksheet.

5 Select the folder you wish to back up, or choose your account to back up everything, then click **Next**

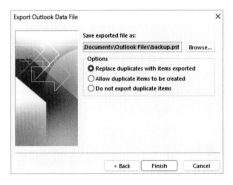

Choosing to back up everything will also export junk mail. Choose only what you really need to back up.

6 Choose a file destination and select a duplication option, then click **Finish**

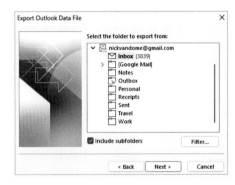

179

7 Enter a password if required, then click **OK** to create a backup file of your chosen file type

To restore your account, simply reverse the procedure by choosing **Import from another program or file** in Step 3 on the previous page, then browse to your backup file.

180

Opening blocked attachments

Viruses transmitted by email are almost always contained in an attachment to the email. However, the attachment must be opened by the user before the virus can be released.

To prevent this, Outlook has a virus protection feature that prevents any attachment it considers unsafe from being opened. When this happens, you will see a message at the top of the email saying that access to the attachment has been blocked. An example of this is shown below:

Outlook can be configured to read email in plain text format. When you enable this setting, no dangerous content in the email is run. Do it as follows:

• From the **File** menu, click **Options** > **Trust Center**, then click the **Trust Center Settings** button.

• Choose **Email Security**, then check the **Read all standard mail in plain text** option.

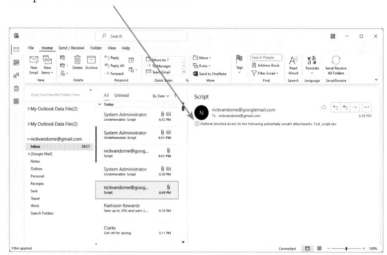

This is all very well, and the feature will prevent people from opening dangerous attachments, either through ignorance or carelessness. However, if you are certain that an attachment is safe – you recognize the sender and know exactly what the attachment is, for example – you may wish to know how to open it.

1 Ensure that the Outlook app is closed

2 In the Windows Search box on the Taskbar, enter **regedit** then click on the **Registry Editor** option, or click on it on the Taskbar, if it has been pinned there

3 Next, navigate to this registry key: **HKEY_CURRENT_USER\SOFTWARE\Microsoft\Office\16.0\Outlook\Security**

Some email providers, such as **Gmail**, prohibit the sender from attaching files that have unsafe file extensions, in an attempt to reduce the spread of malware.

4 Right-click in the right-hand pane and choose **New > String Value**, then precisely name the value **Level1Remove**

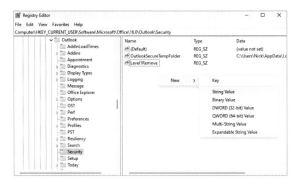

Hot tip

Many antivirus apps have a facility to scan email attachments to detect dangerous files.

5 Double-click on the new value to open the **Edit String** dialog and enter the file extension (including a period) of the blocked file you want to open – for example, **.vbs**

6 Click **OK** to close the **Edit String** dialog, then close the Registry Editor

7 Open the Outlook app and see that access to the attached file is no longer blocked

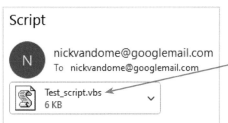

Beware

Here, the file extension of **.vbs** is a Visual Basic Script – a file type that is potentially harmful.

8 Click on the attachment and choose **Save to Disk...** in the **Attachment Security Warning** dialog, then locate the file to freely open it

Hot tip

Refer to the tables on pages 182-183 to discover which file extensions are safe to open and which are not.

9 Close Outlook then re-open the Registry Editor and delete the **Level1Remove** value – to resume blocking

High-risk file attachments

An email attachment ending in any of the file extensions in the table below can, potentially, be carrying a virus:

File extension	Description
.ADE	Microsoft Access Project extension
.ADP	Microsoft Access Project
.BAS	Visual Basic Class module
.BAT	Batch file
.CHM	Compiled HTML help file
.CMD	Windows NT Command Script
.COM	MS-DOS application
.CPL	Control Panel extension
.CRT	Security certificate
.EXE	Application
.HLP	Windows help file
.HTA	HTML application
.INF	Setup information file
.INS	Internet communication settings
.ISP	Internet communication settings
.JS	JScript file
.JSE	JScript Encoded Script file
.LNK	Shortcut
.MDB	Microsoft Access application
.MDE	Microsoft Access MDE database
.MSC	Microsoft Common Console document
.MSI	Windows installer package
.MSP	Windows installer patch
.MST	Visual Test Source file
.PCD	Photo CD image
.PIF	Shortcut to MS-DOS app
.REG	Registry file
.SCR	Screen saver
.SCT	Windows Script Component
.URL	Internet shortcut
.VB	Visual Basic file
.VBE	VBScript Encoded Script file
.VBS	VBScript Script file
.ZIP	Zipped folder

Beware

The extension of a malware file may have been changed in order to disguise it. Be wary of all attachments from unknown sources.

Low-risk file attachments

The file types in this table are extremely unlikely to be carrying a virus and can be considered to be safe:

File extension	Description
.GIF	Picture – Graphics Interchange Format
.TIF or .TIFF	Picture – Tagged Image File Format
.MPEG	Movie – Motion Picture Expert Group
.AVI	Movie – Audio Video Interleaved
.MP3	Sound – MPEG compressed audio
.WAV	Sound – Audio
.TXT or .TEXT	Notepad document
.BMP	Picture – Windows Bitmap
.ICO	Picture – Icon
.PNG	Picture – Portable Network Graphics
.WMF	Picture – Windows Meta File
.LOG	Log file

In an effort to disguise the extension of the file in which the virus is hidden, some virus writers give the file two extensions. The dangerous one is always the last. If you ever get such an attachment, delete it immediately.

Opening blocked images

Another security feature in **Outlook** prevents the automatic download of images within emails that have been included from web pages. In this event, there will be an information text box explaining the issue:

> (i) If there are problems with how this message is displayed, click here to view it in a web browser.
> Click here to download pictures. To help protect your privacy, Outlook prevented automatic download of some pictures in this message.

This protects the user from accessing potentially offensive material and helps to prevent spam. Many spammers include an image URL in their emails that notifies the spammer when the message is opened – confirming that the address is real.

Should the user wish to see the image, they just have to right-click and choose **Download Pictures**. It is also possible to disable the feature in **Outlook** so that all images are shown automatically when the message is opened. Do this by clicking **File** > **Options** then choosing **Trust Center** in the left-hand sidebar. Click the **Trust Center Settings** button, then choose the **Automatic Download** item in the left pane. Now, uncheck the **Don't download pictures automatically in HTML email or RSS items** option.

An attachment extension to be particularly wary of is **.ZIP**. This catches many people out, as most PC users are familiar with the ZIP compression format and see no threat in it.

Managing senders

Most email apps provide the ability to create a list of "safe senders" whose incoming messages you consider trustworthy. Conversely, they also typically let you create a list of "blocked senders" who are deemed untrustworthy. Creating a safe sender list and a blocked sender list helps ensure that a message will not be incorrectly marked as spam when it arrives.

In Outlook, for example, the junk email filter automatically moves suspicious messages to the **Junk Email** folder. Unless you check this regularly, you may fail to notice it has incorrectly moved a message there from a reliable source. Adding that source to the app's **Safe Senders** list would prevent that from happening.

Hot tip

If you receive emails from various trusted sources at the same domain – say, people within the same company domain – you can elect to add the entire domain to the Safe Senders list by choosing **Never Block Sender's Domain** on the Junk menu.

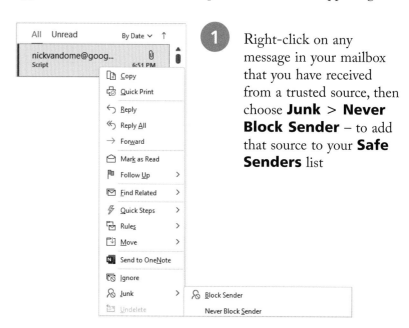

1 Right-click on any message in your mailbox that you have received from a trusted source, then choose **Junk > Never Block Sender** – to add that source to your **Safe Senders** list

2 Click **OK** to close a dialog that confirms the addition

Don't forget

Email addresses and domains in the **Safe Senders** list are never treated as junk email.

3 Next, on the **Home** Ribbon click here and click **Junk E-mail Options...** – to launch the **Junk Email Options** dialog

4 Choose the **Safe Senders** tab to see the trusted source has now been added to the list

Hot tip

You can also use this **Add...** button to manually add the email addresses of trusted sources to the **Safe Senders** list.

Hot tip

Check these options if you want to add sources to the **Safe Senders** list from your **Contacts** list, and people to whom you send messages.

5 Now, choose the **Options** tab, then if you want to restrict incoming messages to strictly only sources on your **Safe Senders** list, check the **Safe Lists Only** option

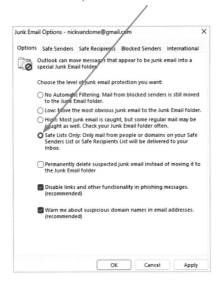

Don't forget

You can select the **Blocked Senders** tab on the **Junk Email Options** dialog to create a list of email addresses you do not trust.

6 Click **Apply** to implement the option, then click **OK** to close the dialog

Once you are on the spammers' lists, the only way of stopping them is to close the account.

Never reply to a spammer. If you do, you will confirm that your address is a real one.

Chatrooms, newsgroups and message boards are favorite places for spammers. Never post your email address on these websites.

A spam-free inbox

Spam accounts for approximately three-quarters of email traffic worldwide. That adds up to several billion emails every day.

If you find yourself the recipient of an endless stream of advertisements, too-good-to-be-true offers, etc., what can you do about it?

The first step is to close your account and then set up a new one – this will stop spam immediately. You then need to make sure the new account is kept out of the spammers' reach. Observing the following rules will help:

● **Make your address as long as possible**. Among other things, spammers use automated generators that churn out millions of combinations (aaa@aol.com, aab@aol.com, and so on). It won't take them long to catch up with bob@aol.com.

● **Never post your address on a website**. Spammers use spiders that trawl the web looking for the @ symbol, which is in all email addresses.

● **If you need to give an address to access a web page, give a false one**. Alternatively, set up a specific account with filters that direct all received emails to the Deleted Items folder. Use this account when an address is asked for.

● **Never click the Unsubscribe from this mailing list link in a received spam email**. This tells the spammer that your address is real and could open the floodgates.

● **Make use of your email app's filters (rules in Outlook)**. Properly configured, these can cut out a lot of spam.

● **Use a Bayesian filter**. This is available as a third-party product and integrates with your email app. Its effectiveness is due to the fact that it is "intelligent", and thus can be trained in much in the same way as voice recognition software.

The Bayesian filter examines all aspects of a message, as opposed to simple keyword checking that classifies a message as spam on the basis of a single word or phrase. Once set up and trained, a Bayesian filter will eliminate 99% of spam.

Organizing your emails

If you're like most people, your inbox will be bulging at the seams with messages from weeks, months and even years ago. This tip shows how to tidy it up and then keep it tidy:

1 Create a new message folder for each of your contacts

2 Go through the inbox and move your messages to the new categorized folders. Delete any you don't want

Having created order out of chaos, you need to make sure it stays that way, and without having to do it manually. To this end, you now need to set up your email app's message filters to do the job automatically.

3 Click the **Home** option on the Ribbon, then select **Rules** > **Manage Rules & Alerts** > **New Rule** – to launch the **Rules Wizard** dialog

4 Choose **Move messages from someone to a folder**

5 Click the **from** item link – to open a dialog where you can select a contact

6 Click the **move it to the** [item] link – to open a dialog where you can select a folder

7 Click **Finish** > **OK**, and from this point on all messages from the specified contact will be moved automatically to the specified folder

A big advantage of organizing your emails in this way is found when you need to locate an old message for re-reading. Instead of having to search through an overflowing inbox, you will know exactly where it is.

You can create multiple email rules but you should be aware that their order is significant. Rules are processed in the order listed – a rule may be overridden by a subsequent rule.

Automatic picture resizing

As anybody who regularly uses email will know, email apps allow users to either insert images directly into an email or attach them as a file, or sometimes both.

The problem with this is that unless the image has been reduced in size in an imaging app (a process of which many people are unsure), it is possible to end up sending a huge picture file that will take the recipient ages to download. Most people find this extremely irritating, as it can occupy their connection for a considerable length of time.

Windows saves the day with its **Email Picture Resizing** utility.

You can resize any number of pictures at the same time – you are not restricted to just one.

1 Right-click the image you want to send with your email, and select **Send to** and then **Mail Recipient**

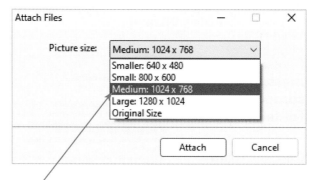

Attach Files	— □ ×
Picture size:	Medium: 1024 x 768 ⌄
	Smaller: 640 x 480
	Small: 800 x 600
	Medium: 1024 x 768
	Large: 1280 x 1024
	Original Size
	Attach Cancel

Beware

Be wary of using the **Small** and **Smaller** resize options. While these reduce the size of files enormously, they also reduce the quality of images considerably.

2 Select the required option – e.g. **Small**, **Medium**, **Original Size**, etc. – and then click **Attach**

3 Click **OK** and an email message window will open with the resized image attached. All you have to do is type in the address and some text before sending the message

A couple of things to be aware of:

- Pictures resized in this way are converted to the **JPEG** format, which you may or may not want.

- Some image formats (Photoshop's **PSD**, for example) cannot be converted by the utility, and thus cannot be resized – they will be attached to the email but at the original size.

Hot tip

Be aware of file formats, as they also determine the size of an image file. For example, a **BMP** file of 4MB may be reduced to 100KB in **JPEG** format!

13 Multimedia

Multimedia has always been one of the most popular uses of PCs. This chapter looks at ways of enhancing your multimedia experience, with music, movies and TV.

Beware

Most codec packs are designed for specific versions of Windows. If you do decide to install one, be sure it is compatible with the Windows version you are using.

Playing any media file

Video and audio files in their raw state are huge in size, so compression techniques are used to reduce their size for downloading and copying. The app that does the compressing is known as a codec (**co**mpressor-**dec**ompressor), and there are lots of them. Two well-known examples are **DIVX** for video and **MP3** for audio. Once a file has been compressed, it must then be decompressed before it can be played. The decompression is done by the same codec that compressed the file originally. This can create a problem for computer users if they have a media file but are unable to play it because the required codec is not installed on their PC. There are a couple of ways to resolve this issue:

● Check the file with an app that will analyze it and tell you which codec is required to play it.

● Install a codec pack, which contains codecs for virtually all types of media files.

Windows 11 provides most commonly-used codecs, but there are still many others. There are several codec packs available on the internet, and if you choose this option we suggest you do a bit of research before installing one. Some of them can cause more problems than they solve. One codec pack that we have evaluated and can recommend is the free **Shark007** codec pack, available for download at **shark007.net/index.html**

This application does just what it says – it installs all the codecs you are ever likely to need, without also installing superfluous features such as bundled media players, etc.

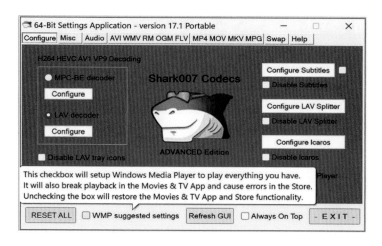

Multimedia viewers

For viewing your pictures, Windows 11 provides the **Photos** app, which has a limited set of features. The powerful **IrfanView** imaging app has a vast range of features and is available for free at **irfanview.com**

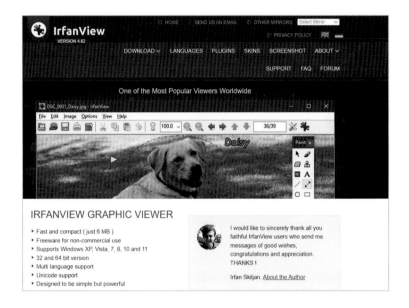

IrfanView has a wide range of functions that can be further extended by downloading free plugins from the manufacturer's website.

For viewing video, Windows 11 provides the excellent **Media Player**, which has a good range of features. Another option is **Zoom Player**, which has an uncluttered interface and is available free at **inmatrix.com** – an excellent free app.

Media Player

The **Media Player** app can be used to play and manage digital music with Windows 11. To use it:

1 Select **Media Player** from the **Start** menu or **All apps** list

2 The Media Player homepage is displayed, with the left-hand sidebar used for navigating around

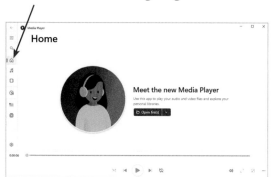

3 Click on this icon (**Music library**) in the sidebar and then choose to list **Songs**, **Albums** (below) or **Artists**. The albums in your music library will be listed in alphabetical sequence and with cover pictures displayed

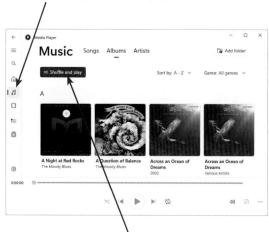

4 Click **Shuffle and play** to listen to tunes, selected randomly from your collection

Hot tip

Media Player is the video and audio player for Windows 11, and replaces the **Groove Music** and **Windows Media Player** apps.

Don't forget

Click on the menu button in the sidebar navigation to display titles for icons.

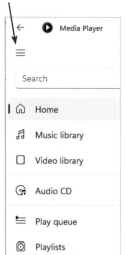

...cont'd

Details of the current track are shown, and the progression is illustrated by a slider at the bottom of the window

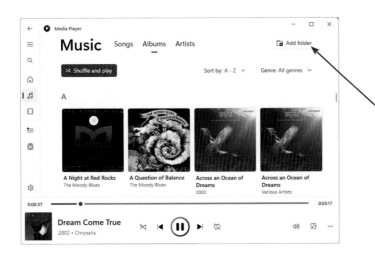

You can click the **Add folder** button to specify another folder that contains music.

5 To change the sequence in which albums are displayed, you should click **Sort by** and then choose an option: **A - Z**, **Release year**, **Artist** or **Date added**

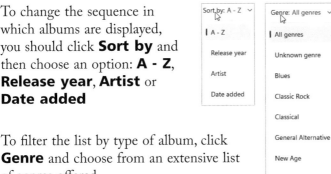

6 To filter the list by type of album, click **Genre** and choose from an extensive list of genres offered

You can play albums that are on your OneDrive on any device where you sign in with your Microsoft account.

7 You can adjust the volume, switch to **Mini player**, or select **More options** (**...**) to display a list of actions that are available

Playing audio CDs

Although playing an audio CD on a computer may seem a little old-fashioned in a world of streaming music, it still plays an important role as there are still many CDs that are used for music. To do this:

1 Insert the audio CD into your computer's CD drive and open the **Media Player** app

2 Click on this button (**Audio CD**) in the left-hand sidebar

3 Details of the audio CD are displayed in the main window

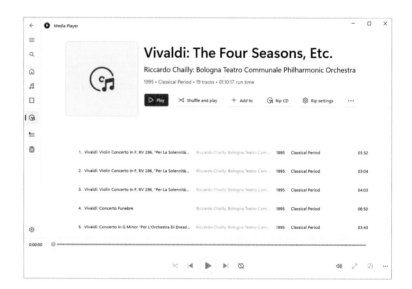

4 Click on a track to select it and click on the **Play** button

5 Click on the **Shuffle and play** button to play the tracks of the CD in random order

6 Click on a track to select it and click on the **Play** button —

7 As a track plays, the music controls are available at the bottom of the window

Hot tip

Drag the slider in Step 7 to move to different points in a track.

8 Use these controls to, from left to right: shuffle the tracks on the CD; go to the start of the current track being played; pause or play the current track; go to the end of the current track; repeat the current track being played

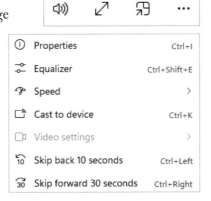

9 Use these controls to, from left to right: change the volume; display **Media Player** in full-screen; minimize the **Media Player** window so that it only takes up a small part of the screen; access the **More options** panel

ⓘ Properties		Ctrl+I
⚏ Equalizer		Ctrl+Shift+E
⌁ Speed		>
⬚ Cast to device		Ctrl+K
▢ Video settings		>
⟲ Skip back 10 seconds		Ctrl+Left
⟳ Skip forward 30 seconds		Ctrl+Right

Beware

Be careful not to set the volume too high for an audio CD, particularly for an extended period of time.

...cont'd

Playing videos

Media Player can also play some videos, and this is excellent for viewing your own videos that have been captured on a smartphone or a digital camera. Once videos have been downloaded to your computer you can then start watching them.

1 Click the **Video library** icon in the left-hand sidebar

2 The available videos are displayed in the **Video** section

3 By default, the videos displayed in **Media Player** are those in the **Videos** folder in **File Explorer**

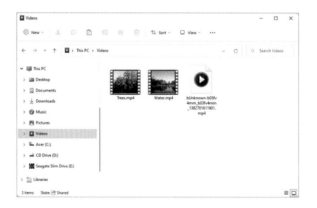

4 Double-click a video to play it and use these buttons to manage the playback of the video

Click the **Add folder** button in Step 2 to add more folders from where videos will be displayed. If more videos are added to these folders they will automatically be displayed in the **Media Play Video** section.

Movies and TV

The **Movies & TV** app can also be used to view and play movies, TV shows and your own videos.

1 Click the **Movies & TV** icon on the **Start** menu to start the app

Don't forget

The **Movies & TV** app supports most DRM-free video formats, including:

.m4v	.mp4
.mov	.asf
.avi	.wmv
.m2ts	.3g2
.3gp2	.3gpp

2 The app opens with **Explore** selected, showing featured movies. Select **Trailers** for more movies

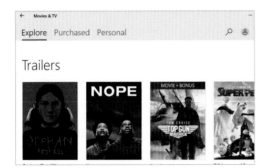

Hot tip

Click the links to see the specified selections, or simply scroll the **Explore** page to see subsets of each.

3 Click the **Personal** tab to see an item of your own that you have saved to the **Movies & TV** app

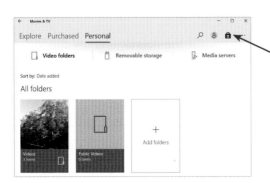

Don't forget

Click the **Microsoft Store** icon to open the Store with **Movies & TV** selected. Review the content, and purchase and download any items that you desire.

Hot tip

Many of the vector formats (including the four mentioned on the right) can also handle raster data. These are often called "metafiles", such as the Windows Metafile format WMF.

Hot tip

You may also encounter the **SVG** (Scalable Vector Graphics) file format. This enables two-dimensional vector images to be displayed in web pages using **XML** (eXtensible Markup Language).

Graphic formats unraveled

When using graphics files in documents, presentations, web pages, or for printing, it is important that you choose a format that is suitable for the task in hand. Using the wrong one can result in poor-quality images, images that take an eternity to open, or images with unnecessarily high file sizes.

The first thing to realize is that image formats are split into two main groups: vector and raster.

Vector

Vector images are composed of mathematically-defined geometric shapes – e.g. lines, squares, circles, etc. – and are typically generated by drawing applications such as Adobe Illustrator and Microsoft Visio. Two notable advantages of this format are:

- The image size can be increased to an almost unlimited degree without noticeable loss of image quality.

- Individual parts of an image can be edited. For example, if a particular image contains both text and objects, it is possible to change the text's formatting – font, color, size, etc.

Vector formats tend to be proprietary; i.e. specific to a particular app. However, many drawing applications allow you to save an image in formats used by other popular vector apps.

Commonly-used vector formats include:

- **WMF** – This is the standard vector file used in Microsoft products, such as Microsoft 365/Office.

- **PCT** – This is the standard vector format used by Apple Mac operating systems.

- **EPS** – This format can be used on a variety of platforms, including Apple Mac and Windows.

- **AI** – This format is the default used by the industry-standard Adobe Illustrator vector graphics drawing application.

Raster

In raster files, the image is comprised of a grid (or matrix) of tiny squares called pixels. This allows extremely complex pictures to be recorded, typically photographs, and it's this characteristic that makes them the most widely-used format.

The main drawback is that in their raw state, raster files can be very large. However, this is compensated for by the fact that this format can be heavily compressed to reduce file size.

With regard to compression, there are two types, lossy and lossless:

- **Lossy** – With this method, unnecessary data is permanently stripped out of the file, thus reducing its size. Although it may be imperceptible, the quality of the image is reduced.

- **Lossless** – Here, data is temporarily removed from the file. When the file is opened, the data is replaced. Thus, there is no loss of image quality.

Commonly-used raster formats are:

- **JPEG** – A lossy format, JPEG's main advantage is the fact that it can be highly compressed. This makes it ideal for use in web pages, and where a low file size is required. It can also handle 24-bit color, and so can be used for professional printing (although there are better formats for this).

- **GIF** – This is a low-size lossless image format that is mostly found on websites where it is used for small low-quality images, such as advertising banners, clip art, etc. Use this format if you want the lowest possible file size and the quality of the image is not important.

- **PNG** – This is an advanced version of the GIF format and it offers several advantages, such as better color support and compression. PNGs are lossless.

- **TIFF** – This is a lossless format offering features that make it the ideal format for professional printing. File sizes are high but image quality is excellent.

Summary

For web pages where quality is not important, or low file size is, use GIF or PNG. Otherwise, use JPEG (a.k.a. JPG).

For general computer use – e.g. storing and viewing your holiday snaps – JPEG is the recommended format.

For professional printing of photographs, use the TIFF format.

Hot tip

There are several variants of the JPEG format. These include JP2000, JPM, and JP3D. These are designed for more specific uses, such as volumetric imaging (JP3D), and usually require a plugin.

Hot tip

If an image contains both drawing objects (vector) and photographs (raster), use a metafile format such as EPS.

Editing your photos

Calibrating the monitor

The first thing you must do is calibrate the monitor. If it is incorrectly set up, no matter how carefully you edit your images, when you print them or view them on a different monitor, they will look different. You may even make them worse. Calibration software should be bundled with your monitor. If not, use the calibration utility provided by Windows – see page 142.

Hot tip

If you have an image that cannot be replaced, make a copy and use that for editing. If you mess it up, you've still got the original.

Converting the image to a lossless format

As shown on page 199, image formats are either lossy or lossless. Every time a lossy image is edited, some loss of image data occurs. Thus, the more times it is edited, the worse the end result. Lossless images, on the other hand, can be edited any number of times with no loss of quality. So, before you edit any image of the lossy type, convert it to **TIFF** format, which is lossless. Having edited the image, convert it back to the original file type. It takes a few seconds and ensures that the original image quality is retained.

Brightness and contrast adjustments

All image editors provide brightness and contrast controls. Many also have an auto one-click setting that does the job automatically. While both can work well, often the result is less than optimal.

A better and more reliable way is to use the image editor's **Histogram** control. This presents a graphical representation of the image showing its color distribution in terms of brightness and darkness. The left of the graph represents black and the right represents white.

Consider the following example of a badly under-exposed picture:

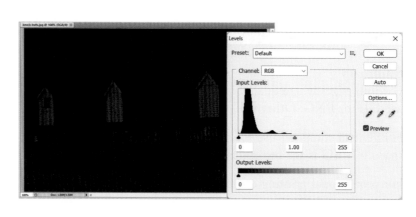

The image's **Histogram** shows that its data is over to the left of the graph; i.e. its dark tones are overemphasized. (If an image's exposure is correct, the data will be centered in the graph.)

1 Drag the white pointer to where the data begins – to set the image's exposure to the correct level

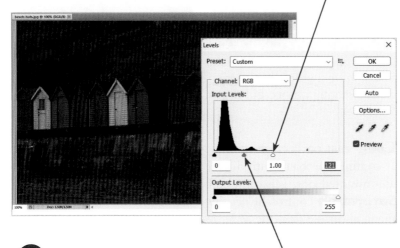

The right pointer controls light tones (highlights), the left one controls dark tones (shadows), and the middle one controls midtones (contrast).

2 Now, drag the gray pointer in the middle – to set the image's contrast to the correct level

Color correction

The next adjustment to make is to the image's colors. This is done with the **Hue/Saturation** control (shown below). A common mistake is to adjust all the colors simultaneously until the picture "looks about right". However, this often results in one color being correct and the others being incorrect.

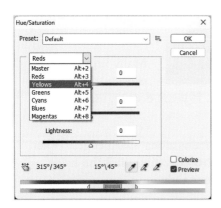

The right way to do it is to edit each color individually by selecting it from the color menu. Adjustments will thus affect that color only.

An example is shown on page 202.

If an image is over exposed, its data will be to the right of the graph. In this case, you would drag the black slider to where the data begins.

Another more advanced tool that can be used for color correction is the **Curves** tool.

...cont'd

Another way to adjust the color of a specific area of an image is to select the area with a selection tool, such as the **Marquee** or **Lasso** tool. Any changes you make will affect the selected area only.

202

Don't forget

Sharpening tools should be used with restraint. Overuse will ruin your images.

In this image, the grass and foliage have a yellowish tint that gives a slightly washed-out or faded look

Adjusting green only gives the grass and foliage a richer color, while the other colors remain unchanged

Color-cast correction

A common problem with digital photos is the image having an unwanted tint. This can also be corrected with the **Hue/Saturation** control. Select the color of the cast in the **Edit** menu and then drag the slider back to eliminate it.

Sharpening

The first rule of image sharpening is that this process is the last edit to be made. The second rule is to ignore the **Sharpen** and **Sharpen More** tools, as they provide little user control and usually result in the image being sharpened incorrectly.

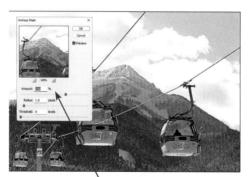

The tool you should use is **Unsharp Mask**. When using this, you need to zoom in closely so that you can work with precision.

Many imaging apps provide a zoom-in preview window for this purpose. If yours doesn't, use the app's zoom control to get in close.

The rule of thumb is to look for halos along sharp edges. When you see these, reduce the **Threshold** setting until the halos disappear, then you should be about right.

14 Miscellaneous

This chapter contains a number of tips that relate to using your Windows 11 PC that may not be obvious at first glance.

Keyboard calculator

The **Calculator** app provided by Windows is a very handy and much-used application. However, operating it with a mouse is less than ideal as it is very easy to press the wrong button. You could never add up a column of figures at anything like the speed of a real calculator.

The tip described below allows you to do just that:

1 Press the **Num Lock** key on the keyboard to activate the numeric keypad

2 Type **calc** into the Taskbar Search box, then hit **Enter** to launch the **Calculator** app

Don't forget

Click the "hamburger" button to switch the **Calculator** app into **Scientific** mode, **Graphing** mode, **Programmer** mode, **Date calculation** mode, or one of its many **Converter** modes.

3 Instead of fiddling about with the mouse to enter numbers, simply use the numeric keypad on the right-hand side of the keyboard

Hot tip

While the **Calculator** app supplied by Windows is perfectly adequate for most needs, there are many more specialized calculators available for download from the internet.

Key	Action
/	The equivalent of divide
*	The equivalent of multiply
+	The equivalent of plus
-	The equivalent of minus
Enter	The equivalent of equals

Restarting Windows Explorer

From time to time **Windows Explorer,** which is the application responsible for the Taskbar and the desktop, will crash. The result is that the Taskbar and all desktop icons will disappear, leaving a blank screen. With nothing to click, the user seemingly has no options with which to recover.

The solution is as follows:

1 Press **Ctrl + Shift + Esc**. This opens **Task Manager**

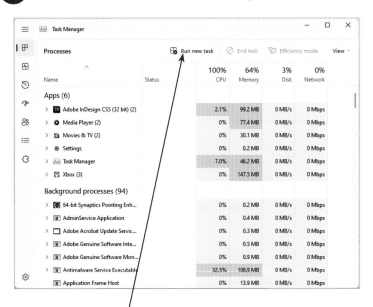

2 Click **Run new task** on the top toolbar

3 In the **Open** box, type **explorer** and then click **OK**

Windows will now restart **Windows Explorer**, which will in turn reinstate the Taskbar and the desktop icons.

To open **Task Manager** when you have no access to the Taskbar, just press **Ctrl + Shift + Esc**.

You can click the **Performance** button in the left-hand sidebar in **Task Manager** to see usage graphs for your CPU, memory, disk, and Wi-Fi.

If a process has "gone rogue", slowing down your PC to a crawl, open **Task Manager** then check the **Processes > CPU** column to select the wayward process and click **End task** to kill that process.

Hot tip

The **Pointers** tab provides a range of mouse pointers that you may find more suitable for your use of the PC than the default pointer.

Don't forget

The **Wheel** tab provides options to adjust horizontal and vertical scrolling actions with the mouse wheel.

Hot tip

Have you ever been in a situation where you have simply lost the pointer? Checking **Show location of pointer when I press the CTRL key** will enable you to find it instantly the next time you lose it.

Turbo-charging the mouse

Many users are not aware that several aspects of the mouse can be enhanced, both visually and operationally.

Pointer speed

The first is the speed at which the pointer moves across the screen. The default setting is fine for most users, but some – gamers, for example – will benefit from a faster speed:

 Go to **Control Panel > Hardware and Sound > Devices and Printers > Mouse**. Then, click the **Pointer Options** tab

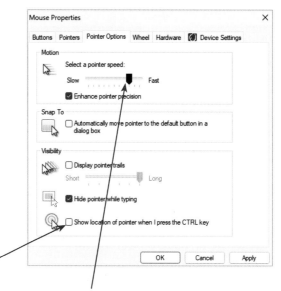

2 Drag the slider forward, and click **Apply** then **OK** to increase the pointer's speed

Mouse Snap To

While you have the **Pointer Options** dialog box open, you can alter another setting that will change the mouse's behavior.

Enabling **Snap To** will, to a certain extent, eliminate the need to move your mouse by making the pointer jump automatically to the default button whenever a new dialog box is opened. Some people love this; others hate it. Give it a try.

Easy reading

The **ClearType** feature is an anti-aliasing technique that smooths the edges of fonts, thus making them easier to read.

It is possible to tweak the level of **ClearType** text. This can be done as described below:

1 Open the **Settings** app and enter **ClearType** into the **Search** box and click on the **Adjust ClearType text** option

> 🖥 Adjust ClearType text

2 At the first screen, click **Next**. At the second, select the monitor to apply the settings to (assuming you have more than one)

3 The next four screens will present you with different **ClearType** options

4 Choose the setting that's best for you, then click **Next** and then **Finish**

Not everybody likes **ClearType**. If you want to disable it, uncheck **Turn on ClearType** on the first screen.

You can also open **ClearType Text Tuner** from the **Run** box with the **cttune** command.

If you have more than one monitor, you can apply different **ClearType** settings to each monitor.

System details

Windows provides a useful tool for users who need to get details about their system.

System Information

This gives detailed information about all the hardware and software on the PC. To open it, go to the Taskbar **Search** box and type **msinfo32.exe**. The main page gives a system summary that details items such as the CPU, the amount of installed memory, operating system, etc.

Device Manager

This utility allows you to view, configure, and troubleshoot your PC's hardware devices. To open it, right-click on the **Start** button and click the **Device Manager** option.

Device Manager lists all your system's hardware. Expanding the categories gives details, and access to the system properties, for individual devices.

Device Manager also flags any devices that are not working with warning symbols, and allows you to install and update device drivers.

Third-party utilities

While **System Information** and **Device Manager** provide a lot of information about the system, there are many third-party utilities that provide greater detail. One of the best is **SiSoftware** (shown below) – available for download at **sisoftware.net**

For really in-depth details about your system, it is a highly-recommended download.

Video and audio codecs

A problem some users encounter when trying to play a video file is that they get sound but no video (or no sound, in the case of a sound file). The reason is that the file's codec (see the Don't forget tip) is missing. To resolve the issue, you need to download and install it. The difficulty is knowing which codec is needed. Go to **headbands.com/gspot** and download an app called **GSpot**. Open the errant file with **GSpot** and you will be told which codec it was compressed with and lots of other information about the file, and you can then do a web search for the required codec.

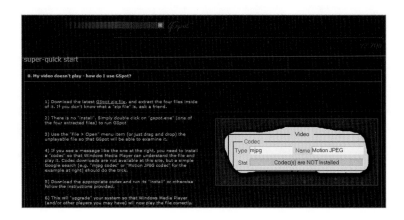

Hot tip

SiSoftware is available in various versions. The **Lite** version, which is free, will give you all the information you need.

Hot tip

Another good utility is **Belarc Advisor**. This is available for free download at **belarc.com**

Don't forget

A codec is an app that compresses the data in sound and video files, thus reducing the size of the files. When the file is played, the same codec must be installed on the PC in order to decompress it.

You must run **Steps Recorder** as an administrator in elevated mode to record any activities that need administrator authority.

Some apps – for example, a full-screen game – might not be captured accurately or provide useful details.

Steps Recorder

If you are the local PC guru, you're probably resigned to friends and family pestering you for help with their computer problems. This is bad enough, but when they are unable to clearly explain what the problem is or what they've done – as is often the case – it becomes very difficult, or even impossible, to help them.

A little-known utility supplied with Windows 11 may provide the answer. When you get one of these irritating phone calls, tell the caller to go to their PC, type **psr** into the Taskbar **Search** box and press **Enter**. This will open the Windows 11 **Steps Recorder**.

Once they have this running, get them to press **Start Record** and reproduce the fault or do whatever it was they did, again. **Steps Recorder** will capture every mouse click and keystroke. When they've finished, they press **Stop Record** and a report is generated and saved as a **ZIP** file. This can then be emailed to you. When you open the report, you will see a detailed step-by-step list of every action that was made. Even more helpful is the fact that screenshots are included, as shown below:

This is useful for the reverse situation as well – trying to explain how to do something to the user. A series of screenshots indicating where to click will be much easier for an inexperienced user to follow.